BestMasters

Mit „**BestMasters**" zeichnet Springer die besten Masterarbeiten aus, die an renommierten Hochschulen in Deutschland, Österreich und der Schweiz entstanden sind. Die mit Höchstnote ausgezeichneten Arbeiten wurden durch Gutachter zur Veröffentlichung empfohlen und behandeln aktuelle Themen aus unterschiedlichen Fachgebieten der Naturwissenschaften, Psychologie, Technik und Wirtschaftswissenschaften. Die Reihe wendet sich an Praktiker und Wissenschaftler gleichermaßen und soll insbesondere auch Nachwuchswissenschaftlern Orientierung geben.

Springer awards "**BestMasters**" to the best master's theses which have been completed at renowned Universities in Germany, Austria, and Switzerland. The studies received highest marks and were recommended for publication by supervisors. They address current issues from various fields of research in natural sciences, psychology, technology, and economics. The series addresses practitioners as well as scientists and, in particular, offers guidance for early stage researchers.

More information about this series at http://www.springer.com/series/13198

Patricia Dörr

The Impact of Monetary Policy on Economic Inequality

With a Preface by Prof. Dr. Matthias Neuenkirch

Springer Gabler

Patricia Dörr
Trier, Germany

ISSN 2625-3577 ISSN 2625-3615 (electronic)
BestMasters
ISBN 978-3-658-24834-5 ISBN 978-3-658-24835-2 (eBook)
https://doi.org/10.1007/978-3-658-24835-2

Library of Congress Control Number: 2018965239

Springer Gabler

This Springer Gabler imprint is published by the registered company Springer Fachmedien Wiesbaden GmbH part of Springer Nature
The registered company address is: Abraham-Lincoln-Str. 46, 65189 Wiesbaden, Germany

Preface

In her master's thesis, Patricia Dörr studies theoretically and empirically the relationship between monetary policy on the one hand as well as income and expenditure inequality on the other hand. Her remarkable contribution is the extension of the models by JIN (2009) and JIN (2010) that explain economic growth, inflation, and inequality in a unified framework. Ms Dörr relaxes some of the model's strict assumptions and offers a more realistic view on the interdependencies between the aforementioned variables. In particular, her modification proves to be helpful in illustrating the impact of monetary policy on income inequality. In a second step, Ms Dörr puts her model's implications to an empirical test using data for the United States. In line with the existing literature, she finds ambiguous effects of monetary policy on inequality—a result that also fits the predictions of her theoretical analysis.

Ms Dörr's thesis is a contribution to the academic literature that exceeds common expectations on a master's thesis. Her work does not only close a gap in the literature. She also offers a theoretical framework that can be utilized and extended in the current debate about income and wealth inequality and the consequences thereof. I hope that Ms Dörr's work gets the properly deserved attention in academic and political debates.

Trier, September 2018
Prof. Dr. Matthias Neuenkirch

Contents

Page

1 Introduction 1
2 Monetary Policy 5
3 General Equilibrium Models 9
3.1 New Keynesian Models 9
3.2 Classical Monetary Models 10
4 Introducing Agent Heterogeneity 13
5 Combining General Equilibrium Models and Agent Heterogeneity 17
5.1 Model Set-up 17
5.2 Equilibrium - The Balanced Growth Path 22
5.3 Stability of the Income Distribution 26
5.4 Monetary Policy and Inequality 29
5.4.1 The Impact of a Nominal Interest Rate Change 29
5.4.2 Stability of the Balanced Growth Path 34
5.5 Labor Market Segmentation 35
6 Empirical Evidence 39
6.1 Previous Findings 39
6.2 Own Course of Action 41
6.2.1 Methodology and Data 41
6.2.2 Results 48
7 Conclusion 55
References 57
Appendices 61
A Skill, Interest and Wage Change 61
B Proof that $\frac{\dot{E}}{E} = 0$ 61
C Average Education Spending 62
D Time Series Plots 63
E Regression Results 66
F Impulse Response Functions 69

List of Figures

Page

5.1 Relationship between Sector 1 Production and Capital Accumulation 21
5.2 Stability of the BGP 35
6.1 Illustration of the QSR 43
6.2 Time Series of the Yield Curve 47
6.3 Financial Obligation Ratio of Households 49
6.4 IRF of Yield on Gini-Inc 50
6.5 IRF of Yield on Gini-Exp 50
6.6 IRF of Yield on log Variance-Inc 51
6.7 IRF of Inflation on log Variance-Inc 51
6.8 Time Series of Income Quantiles 52
6.9 Lorenz Curve of Income 52
C.1 Education Spending in OECD Countries, Percent of GDP 62
D.1 Share of Population that Completed at least 4 Years of Highschool - First and Second Differences 63
D.2 GDP Growth 63
D.3 Unemployment Rate 63
D.4 GDP Deflator Based Inflation Rate 64
D.5 GINI Coefficient Based on Household Income 64
D.6 RMPG Based on Household Income 64
D.7 log QSR Based on Household Income 64
D.8 log Variance of Household Income 65
D.9 GINI Coefficient Based on Total Household Expenditure 65
D.10 RMPG Based on Total Household Expenditure 65
D.11 log QSR Based on Total Household Expenditure 65
D.12 log Variance of Total Household Expenditure 66
F.1 IRF of Yield on RMPG-Inc 69
F.2 IRF of Yield on log QSR-Inc 69
F.3 IRF of Yield on RMPG-Exp 70
F.4 IRF of Yield on log QSR-Exp 70
F.5 IRF of Yield on log Variance-Exp 70
F.6 IRF of Inflation on log Variance-Exp 70

List of Tables

Page

6.1 Correlation Table of Inequality Measures 45
6.2 Regression on Gini-Inc 50
6.3 Regression on Gini-Exp 53
A.1 Correlation Table - Skill, Interest and Wage Change 61
E.1 Regression on RMPG-Inc 66
E.2 Regression on log QSR-Inc 67
E.3 Regression on log Variance-Inc 67
E.4 Regression on RMPG-Exp 68
E.5 Regression on log QSR-Exp 68
E.6 Regression on log Variance-Exp 69

List of Abbreviations

ADF	Augmented Dickey Fuller test
AIC	Akaike Information Criterion
BC	Budget Constraint
BGP	Balanced Growth Path
CDF	Cumulative Density Function
CES	Consumer Expenditure Survey
CIA	Cash-in-Advance Constraint
CPI	Consumer Price Index
DSGE	Dynamic Stochastic General Equilibrium
FOR	Financial Obligation Ratio
GDP	Gross Domestic Product
IES	Intertemporal Elasticity of Substitution
IRF	Impulse-Response Function
IT	Inflation Targeting
NK	New Keynesian
OG	Overlapping Generation
PPI	Producer Price Index
PT	Price-level Targeting
PUM	Public Use Microdata
QSR	Quintile Share Ratio
RMPG	Relative Median Poverty Gap
VAR	Vector Autoregressive Regression

1 Introduction

Since the Great Recession, the interest on the relationship between monetary policy and economic inequality among households is re-newed (COIBION et al. (2012), BIVENS (2015)). One version is that agent heterogeneity in terms of income and skill affect the macroeconomic outcome of monetary policy (GORNEMANN et al. (2012), AUCLERT (2014) and KAPLAN et al. (2016)). I.e., inequality is considered to be a channel through which monetary policy works on the real sphere. However, the very own effect of monetary policy on (the development of) inequality is subject to controversy, too, (BIVENS, 2015). Both, the complexity of theoretical models that are often only numerically solvable (e.g. DOEPKE et al. (2015)) and the ambiguous empirical evidence (DAVTYAN, 2016) may contribute to the ongoing discussion.

Several times, a positive correlation between inflation (which is in most models a result of monetary policy) and inequality has been found empirically (ROMER and ROMER (1998), ALBANESI (2002)). However, to disentangle causal channels with possible contrary signs (COIBION et al., 2012), has resulted in contrary statements (e.g. COIBION et al. (2012), DAVTYAN (2016) and SAIKI and FROST (2014)). An additional distintion between (possibly contrary) short-term and long term effects of monetary policy on inequality complicates the analysis further.

There are two possible directions of causality between monetary policy and inequality. The first considers monetary policy/inflation as the outcome of a bargaining problem among heterogeneous agents with diverging bargaining power (KANE and MORISETT (1993), ALBANESI (2002)), whereas the second seeks to find arguments for causality into the other direction (JIN (2009), LEE (2010) for consumption dispersion): Different endowments with capital and skill lead to diverging optimal behavior of agents and therefore to a change in the original income dispersion in the aftermath of monetary policy.

The second line of argumentation shall be the focus of this work. Different intertemporal substitution behavior and the heterogeneous composition of income with respect to rental and labor income are two plausible channels through which monetary policy can affect inequality.

The analysis of monetary policy and economic inequality, the latter being counted as part of an economy's real sphere, clashes with the assumption of the (super-)neutrality of money. When currency is considered as an instrument of value storage or (obligatory) payment mean, then money matters. The New Keynesian (NK) literature that seeks to explain the non-neutral role that money plays in the economy, has focused more on the introduction of utility generated from the payment service that money provides, and/or frictions. This means that rather market mechanisms than agent heterogeneity are consulted in order to explain the relevance of money in the

P. Dörr, *The Impact of Monetary Policy on Economic Inequality*,
BestMasters, https://doi.org/10.1007/978-3-658-24835-2_1

real sphere, leading to the basic New Keynesian Model (GALÍ, 2015, chap. 3) with one representative agent and some sort of price rigidity.

Nevertheless, there are other model frameworks that analyse economic inequality and monetary policy, too. JIN (2009) manages to construct an endogenous growth model where money growth is linked to income inequality, even when interaction takes place on markets without frictions. The simplicity of his model allows an analytic solution of the equilibrium, and thus statements are possible that do not depend on specific parameter choices. Many other general equlibrium frameworks that deal with income distributions, especially Dynamic Stochastic General Equilibriums (DSGEs) only have a numerical solution (DOEPKE et al. (2015), KAPLAN et al. (2016), HEER and MAUSSNER (2009, chap. 7)). Therefore, model calibration for the parameter setting is required. This, however, leaves open the question whether the derived results are general findings due to the model set-up or due to the specific parameter vector employed in the simulations. This is one reason why this thesis focuses on a rather simple endogenous growth model with an analytical solution in its main section.

The aspect of different economic sectors, their diverging capital use and consequently the different reactions of sector-specific wage following a monetary policy action, has barely found consideration in the theoretic inequality literature. A further development of JIN (2009), though, analyses a two-sector endogenous growth model (JIN, 2010), but with a competitive labor market. The introduction of a second sector partially reverses the findings of JIN (2009). However, the model expansion with the second economic sector is bought with a simplification at another place: In JIN (2010), labor supply is inelastic in contrast to JIN (2009). On the empirical side, IBRAHIM (2005) finds diverging reactions of economic sectors to monetary shocks in Malaysia, which suggests that in reality, where labor markets are usually segmented, this will generate another income distribution effect.

Another point not mentioned so far is that agents may face entry costs to financial markets or simply cannot bear the failure risk of higher return assets (GREENWOOD and JOVANOVIC, 1989). Hence, until they have saved enough to make the market entry, their capital growth will be slower than that of richer agents. Furthermore, those households would hold more low-interest assets and/or cash relative to their income and are, consequently, more vunerable to peaks on inflation.

This thesis seeks to contribute to the findings about monetary policy and its impact on inequality. First, it is discussed what to expect from the rather abstract notion of "monetary policy" in the subsequent of the thesis. Second, models are discussed that argue for non-neutrality of money and a causal relation between monetary policy and inequality. To that purpose, classical monetary policy models are overviewed. Then, agent heterogeneity is introduced. The first of the two main sections of the thesis introduces a (theoretical) endogenous growth model to analytically uncover the relationship between monetary policy and inequality. Because JIN (2009) and JIN (2010) provide analytical solutions and do not include the arguable model component of price stickiness (WILLIAMSON, 2008), the model set-up is inspired by their work. After the determination of the Balanced Growth Path (BGP), I analyze the effect of an interest rate/inflation shock on both, the stability of the BGP and on the income variance. Briefly, I discuss possible implications of labor market segmentation in the introduced model. An empirical analysis follows. The ambiguous effect of monetary policy on inequality that is analytically shown seems to rule the empirical analysis, too. There is no clear-cut positive or negative effect across the different inequality measures nor across the measures based on household income or expenditure. The final section concludes.

2 Monetary Policy

Under monetary policy, one understands the adjustment of money supply. This is done in order to either "achieve some combination of inflation and output stabilization" (MATHAI, 2009) or, more generally, to target either a certain level of a specific (nominal) interest rate - the refinancing rate - or the monetary base (BOFINGER et al., 2001, pp. 63). The latter defined objective of monetary policy is more general as it lets open the question whether and if so, how monetary policy affects the real sphere measured by macroeconomic variable such as Gross Domestic Product (GDP) and the unemployment rate. Money is monopolistically supplied by a monetary authority, usually a central bank.

In a classical monetary model with one representative agent, monetary policy only changes the price level, i.e. the numeraire of the value of output (GALÍ, 2015). Relative prices and thus the relative valuation of goods and services remain unaffected. Therefore, monetary policy has no impact on the real sphere of the economy, it is neutral.

The introduction of (price) rigidities in the goods market and frictions in the money market create a link between real and nominal sphere of an economy. I come back to the modelling of rigidities and frictions in the next section where NK models, the working horse of current monetary policy analysis (LEE, 2010), are introduced. Additionally, economic models seeking to uncover such a link often introduce some sort of necessity for agents to hold currency. Such necessity may be of the form of "real money in the utility function" (GALÍ, 2015), or the requirement to pay goods in cash, Cash-in-Advance Constraints (CIAs), (JIN, 2009). Possibly, payment service/ value transaction costs are assumed (LEE, 2010), or goods are splitted into cash and credit goods (ALBANESI, 2002). Finally, agents may not have perfect foresight in a dynamic model framework. If money matters e.g. for the reasons given above, and agents act on the basis of prediction errors concerning monetary policy/the price level etc. money might have a (transitory) effect on the real sphere, too. This effect could be aggravated by e.g. asymmetric penalty functions because agents might be risk-averse.

In reality, private institutions serve as intermediary between the monetary authority and other economic agents. Given such a link between the nominal and the real sphere of an economy, those institutions may generate a multiplier effect on the interventions of the monetary authority: In the case of expansionary monetary policy, the financial institution withholds a reserve of the credits received from the monetary authority and re-rents the rest, hence generating a second round of lending that increases the total circulation of money (BOFINGER et al., 2001, chap. 3). Although some economic models incorporate those intermediation services (e.g. GERTLER and KARADI (2009), GREENWOOD and JOVANOVIC (1989)), most models that analyze the impact of monetary policy disregard them and simply give a rule under which either the nominal money

P. Dörr, *The Impact of Monetary Policy on Economic Inequality*,
BestMasters, https://doi.org/10.1007/978-3-658-24835-2_2

supply or the nominal interest rate evolve. Those models are the main focus in the following sections. The introduced model in section 5 ignores financial intermediaries, too.

There are different rules which a monetary authority may follow in order not to act at the board's discretion, but on the base of macroeconomic variables. A well-known rule, which monetary authorities have more or less followed in the last decades, is the *Taylor rule* (GALÍ, 2015, eq. (3.26)):

$$i_t = \rho + \phi_\pi \pi_t + \phi_y (y_t - y^n) + \varepsilon_t, \tag{2.1}$$

where i_t is the nominal interest rate at (discrete) time point t, π_t denotes inflation and $y_t - y^n$ is log output's deviation from the steady state. The idiosyncratic shock ε_t may follow an AR(1) process. ε_t is interpreted as an expansionary (contractionary) monetary policy shock when its sign is negative (positive). Found in economic models, the intercept ρ corresponds to the logarithmic discount rate of a representative agent which should equalize the real interest rate r_t^n in the steady state. The output gap results from price rigidities. NK models that include a Taylor rule have an unique equilibrium for an appropriate choice of the parameters ϕ_π and ϕ_y. For real world application, the Taylor rule must be adapted because neither the expected time discount rate of agents, nor the economy's steady state expressed by y^n is kown.

In empirical research, assuming that a monetary authority follows such a rule allows to run regressions whose residuals can be interpreted as unexpected monetary shock, i.e. the part of monetary policy that rational agents cannot adapt to in advance. The original model to determine these "Romer residuals" is similar to the Taylor rule: It seeks to explain the change of the Federal Funds Rate by its original level, and forecasts of inflation, output growth and the unemployment rate (ROMER and ROMER, 2004). While this measure of monetary policy is rather a measure of policy adjustment errors, it circumvents the problem that rational expectations lead to an a priori adjustment of the agents' behvavior and thus, monetary policy impact is hard to measure. However, this approach is subject to model specifications.

From the deterministic interest rate setting i_t, the equilibrium amount of money follows endogenously (BOFINGER et al., 2001, chap. 3) and vice versa. The policy rule (2.1), using r_t^n instead of ρ, returns zero inflation and output gap (GALÍ, 2015, chap. 4). Furthermore, note that the use of an interest rate i_t as measure of monetary policy is a useful simplification of the transmission process in economic models to be discussed later. Indeed, a change in inflation/the nominal interest rate is interpreted as monetary policy in the model in section 5, too. In fact, the monetary authority rather controls the short-term interest rate, which has, in its turn, an impact on several differentiated interest rates (BOFINGER et al., 2001, chap. 4). Originally, equation (2.1) included the US

Federal Funds Rate as such a short-term interest instead of a more or less unspecific nominal interest rate.

The Fisherian equation

$$i_t = \mathrm{E}_t(\pi_{t+1}) + r_t, \tag{2.2}$$

(GALÍ, 2015, eq. (2.22)) underlines how the nominal sphere, i_t and the expected inflation for the next period, $t+1$, given information in t, relates to the real interest rate r_t. Assuming that equilibrium relative, i.e. real prices, amongst them the interest rate r_t are endogenously determined, the nominal interest rate reflects inflation expectations: When prices are assumed to increase more sharply, savers will demand a higher nominal interest in order to outweigh the loss of value. However, the function could be read in the opposite direction, too: A change in the nominal interest rate may cause a re-adjustment of inflation expectations, too, given r_t.

The (empirical) Taylor rule is in stark contrast to the Friedman rule which requires that

$$i_t = 0 \tag{2.3}$$

(DA COSTA and WERNING, 2008). As currency holdings have the opportunity costs of foregone rents, a positive nominal interest rate can be interpreted as taxation of money. Poorer households have in general a smaller labor income and fewer holdings of assets. In absolute terms, their holdings of cash is smaller, too, while they tend to hold more currency relative to their income (KANE and MORISETT, 1993). Hence, under the model in DA COSTA and WERNING (2008), the authors show that a (nonlinear) labor income tax is Pareto superior to $i_t > 0$ under redistributive considerations. This result, however, could imply that contractionary monetary intervention (which according to equation (2.1) goes along with an increase in i_t) does not reduce income equality in the economy.

Another interesting implication of the Taylor rule (2.1), which must be taken into account in the latter empirical analysis, is the following: A non-zero coefficient ϕ_y makes monetary policy react on booms and busts of real production. As the debate on the relationship between economic growth and inequality is an even more historic one (consider, for example, the ongoing discussion about the Kuznet curve, e.g. in DEININGER and SQUIRE (1998)), an empirical validation of the monetary policy impact on the income distribution must control for economic growth.

Alternatively to a monetary growth rule or an interest rate rule, the monetary authority can target inflation or the price level (MEH et al., 2008). A combination of equations (2.1) and (2.2) would be a way to set an Inflation Targeting (IT) rule that is of a Taylor-type, too: Replace the left hand side of (2.1) with the right hand side of (2.2) and solve for $\mathrm{E}_t(\pi_t)$. In contrast to IT, Price-level Targeting (PT) takes into account past deviations from the envisaged level, it is a policy rule with memory. PT seeks to hold prices at a pre-determined level and hence requires intervention that is different from interest rate rules or IT: With IT, every period matters in itself, but past adjustment errors do not matter for the monetary authority's decision in the current one. When the authority follows PT, however, then it must eradicate past policy mistakes. This has a distributional impact, too, because nominal bonds that are paid back at a given date have consequently a lower real value under IT where side-steps from the planned evolution are unpleasant but will not influence the policy in subsequent periods. However, the distributional effects in MEH et al. (2008) are also due to the exogenously set asset portfolio that differs for different population classes.

In a post-Keynesian framework, ROCHON and SETTERFIELD (2007) discuss several alternative interest rules. The *activist* rule enriches the Taylor rule with other macroeconomic controls, whereas the three introduced *parking-it* approaches aim to control the interest rate, too, but for another purpose: The Smithin rule advocates "low but still positive real interest rates" (ROCHON and SETTERFIELD, 2007) in order to restrict the income of rentiers. The Kansas City rule, in contrast, requires the *nominal* interest rate to equal zero. This is equivalent to the Friedman rule, however, the motivation is different: A zero rate is considered to be natural because it occured in the economy if the monetary authority would not pay any interests to drain excess reserves (ROCHON and SETTERFIELD, 2007). A third parking approach is of interest, too: The "fair" interest rule of Pasinetti wants the real interest rate to evolve with the change of wage growth in order to maintain the income distribution between working and rentier class (ROCHON and SETTERFIELD, 2007). However, note that the macroeconomic model introduced in ROCHON and SETTERFIELD (2007) lacks a microfoundation that would prove the stabilatory character of Pasinetti's rule.

3 General Equilibrium Models

3.1 New Keynesian Models

The main characteristic of a basic NK model is the introduction of price stickiness in the production sector. In order to achieve this, NK models include two market imperfections: First, price rigidities require firms not to be price takers, hence some type of market power has to be introduced. Usually, this leads to the design of monopolistic competition models. Firms produce one variety of a single consumption good and households allocate their resources among those goods of similar pattern because they "love variety". The households' aggregate consumption in the utility function is set to the Dixit-Stiglitz shape analogously to (3.1).

Such a model can be found, e.g. in GALÍ (2015, chap. 3). However, an alternative version is that agents rather consume one final good. In that setting, the production sector is separated into final and intermediate production, where the former is a Dixit-Stiglitz aggregate of intermediate goods that employ the production factors (e.g. LEE (2010), DOEPKE et al. (2015), GORNEMANN et al. (2012)). The Dixit-Stiglitz type of aggregation for a continuum of varieties $x(i)$ on the unit interval is of the form

$$x = \left(\int_0^1 x^{\frac{\sigma-1}{\sigma}}(i)\mathrm{d}i \right)^{\frac{\sigma}{\sigma-1}}, \qquad \sigma \neq 1 \tag{3.1}$$

where $x(i)$ stands either for a variety of a consumption good in the first or an intermediate production good in the second version described. σ is the elasticity of substitution, either between the varieties or in the production using intermediate goods. The substitution elasticity parallels the price elasticity for good $x(i)$. This returns an aggregate price index P_t of

$$P_t = \left(\int_0^1 P_t(i)^{1-\sigma}\mathrm{d}i \right)^{\frac{1}{1-\sigma}}. \tag{3.2}$$

Monopolistic competition has the same implications, be it when applied to a variety of consumption goods or to the aggregation of intermediate goods.

Even without the introduction of further price rigidities, the monopolistic character, i.e. the (limited) market power, allows the firms to set a price that is above marginal production costs. In general, the mark-up turns out to be multiplicative to the marginal costs and to be a function of the price elasticity of demand.

In addition to the monopolistic competition component, impediments in the price setting are designed. These can take the form of adjustment costs, meaning that firms that wish to change their price face costs for doing so. In order to have postive costs for both directions of price adjustment, a functional that is quadratic in the relative

P. Dörr, *The Impact of Monetary Policy on Economic Inequality*,
BestMasters, https://doi.org/10.1007/978-3-658-24835-2_3

price change is employed in the literature (GORNEMANN et al. (2012), KAPLAN et al. (2016)). The Calvo price setting - that is a random survival time of the current price - is commonly employed in the literature, too (GALÍ (2015), LEE (2010)). This means that a firm that has set its price P_t in period t is bound to the decision in the successive period with probability θ. Consequently, each firm maximizes its deflated profit with respect to $P_t(i)$ under the possiblity that it has to stick to that price. Then, inflation is

$$\pi_t = \left(\theta + (1-\theta)\left(\frac{P_t^\star}{P_{t-1}}\right)^{1-\sigma}\right)^{\frac{1}{1-\sigma}}, \tag{3.3}$$

with $\pi_t = 1$ corresponding to zero inflation and for good i, $P_t^\star(i) = P_t^\star$ because all agents are subject to the same function (3.1). The optimal price $P_t^\star$ in period t, is a function of the expected evolvement of marginal costs in $\tau \geq t$, price stickiness θ and the consumers' discount rate (GALÍ, 2015). The expected marginal costs, in their turn, can deviate from the observed marginal costs for two reasons: One, GALÍ (2015) introduces a stochastic process to the technology scaling parameter in the production function. Two, in the case of a Dixit-Stiglitz utility function, competitors stochastically adjust their prices, small deviations from the expectation are possible and consequently the demand that firm i has to meet varies and thus its production.

As far as (real) money demand is concerned, it can be excluded from the utility function in NK models, in contrast to most of the classical monetary models. The reason is that goods demand is now a function of price (indices) and thus incorporates inflation. Hence, payment requires more or less explicitly money so that there is money demand, the more the higher the inflation (3.3). In the classical monetary model, however, there is neither monopolistic competition nor price stickiness and therefore, at each period, change of the relative prices is equal among markets. This is not the case presented here as the aggregate price index is nonlinear in the individual prices, cf. equation (3.2).

There is much more that could be said about NK models. However, derivations of aggregate relations such as the NK Phillips curve or the dynamic IS equation (GALÍ, 2015) are in the following less relevant as the focus lies rather on distributional effects of monetary policy than on its impact on macroeconomic output.

3.2 Classical Monetary Models

Introducing monopolistic competition together with price stickiness is not the only way to model a link between real and nominal sphere of the economy. In the following, models that do not rely on the previously described mechanism in order to establish interdependencies between monetary policy and inequality, are referred to as classical monetary models. Those models focus on money as an asset (e.g. PALIVOS (2004), LONGARETTI et al. (2006)) or interpret it mainly as a payment device (JIN (2009), JIN (2010)).

PALIVOS (2004) and LONGARETTI et al. (2006) apply an Overlapping Generation (OG) model. PALIVOS (2004) abstracts from a production sector and makes money supply relevant to the economy by making it an asset whose nominal return is a function of inflation. In addition, he designs to different type of agents, altruists - who bequest their descendants - and egoists who do not. Consequently, egoists are indifferent between nominal rental income from savings and cash holdings as long as the marginal return is the same. Thus, nominal money growth - inflation - must be positive when the interest rate is alike. Altruists, on the contrary, do not want their bequests to lose value, hence disapprove positive inflation, i.e. they would prefer a monetary policy orientated to the Friedman rule. Conciliation of both interests leads to a weighted mean and hence positive optimal inflation, though the specific rate depends on the composition between altruists and egoists.

Equivalently, LONGARETTI et al. (2006) designs altruistic agents, and money is the unique available asset. However, all agents are altruistic and heterogeneity results rather from two different occupational choices: Agents are randomly endowed with investment ideas of diverging return. Some agents with valuable project ideas hence become entrepreneur as their project return is higher than labor income. A non-degenerated distribution of bequests follows from the two differently paid occupational choices, worker or entrepreneur. Hence, wealth inequality carries on to the next generation, inducing a second source of heterogeneity. Inflation impacts the life time budget constraint and thus makes old agents reallocate their budget between consumption and bequests. Even when the reallocation is proportionally equal accross the two population groups, which occurs under identical preference functions, this keeps only the distribution's first moment constant. The second moment changes, as it is non-linear. Taking the second moment to be an indicator of inequality, the distributional effect of monetary policy follows.

Another suggestion how to model monetary policy with possibly distributional impact is given in WILLIAMSON (2008). The author argues that price stickiness is an overestimated factor in the analysis of monetary policy. Backed by survey data, his result on the non-neutrality of money comes from market segmentation. Households of the model environment have identical preferences (up to a stochastic preference shock) but are split up into two groups. One group that is active on the financial market is directly affected by money supply from the monetary authority. The other group, in contrast, experiences monetary policy only via goods market interaction with the former. Hence, money trickles to the whole of the economy through the intensity of exchange between both groups. All those classical monetary models have in common that they lead to an analytically solvable equilibrium, which is rarely the case for NK once that agent heterogeneity is introduced as it is discussed in the next section.

Yet another approach that derives analytically the distributional impact of monetary policy is the framework of endogeneous growth models. JIN (2009) and JIN (2010) randomly assign intial capital and skill endowment to infinitely lived agents. Money comes into play not by the inclusion in the utility function, but by imposition of a CIA. The monetary policy does neither consist of a Taylor type rule nor an inflation target but of a nominal money growth plan. The consequent inflation impacts negatively real money holdings which are necessary to consume. In JIN (2009), where labor is supplied elastically, more leisure is consumed and wages increase, on which individual skill endowment serves as a multiplier. On the other side, inflation lowers the real return on capital that is unequally distributed, too. In consequence, this means that the overall effect of monetary policy depends on the composition of income dispersion. This ambiguous result may explain the unclear empirical evidence when different time periods an countries are studied.

JIN (2010) expands the model of JIN (2009) in that the paper introduces a second economic sector and the possibility of human capital/skill accumulation. However, the increased complexity in this regard makes the author abolish the assumption of elastic labor supply. The skill accumulation underlies a CIA, too, and consequently, a raise in money growth that implies increased inflation lowers the real money balance. Thus, skill accumulation is lowered and the economy's educational sector loses weight relative to the other production sector. When the latter uses capital more intensively, the contribution of capital share heterogeneity among households becomes more important in total income disparity. Hence, the effect of monetary policy on income inequality again depends on the relative importance of capital and skill inequality. However, note that the findings in JIN (2010) are reverse to those in JIN (2009): In the former, dominance of physical capital heterogeneity leads to a positive effect of expansionary monetary policy on inequality. In the latter, it is the other way around.

General equilibrium models require the simultaneous handling of multiple markets which makes their analytical solution more complicated than partial market equilibria. However, their advantage is that they take into account interdependencies between markets, in their most basic form between labor and goods market. The introduction of agent heterogeneity additionally increases complexity. This might be one of the reasons why the models introduced here model closed economies. However, the consideration of a small open economy would be interesting, too, as the evolution of the price level can affect the exchange rate, as shown for the representative agent case in GALI and MONACELLI (2005). Even when international financial markets are ignored, this influences economic sectors open to trade in the considered economy. In return, an impact on the factor prices and hence on income is thinkable.

4 Introducing Agent Heterogeneity

Under agent heterogeneity will be understood the heterogeneity of consumers or households, which are taken as equivalent terms. Although some attempts to include different economic sectors have been made (e.g. GERTLER and KARADI (2009), DOEPKE et al. (2015), JIN (2010)), those research paths usually delimited themselves to the introduction of financial intermediaries that manage the households' savings (e.g GREENWOOD and JOVANOVIC (1989), GERTLER and KARADI (2009), KAPLAN et al. (2016), GORNEMANN et al. (2012)). When a continuum of firms are introduced, they are usually intermediary firms that produce the input for the final consumption good in the sense of equation (3.1). The symmetry of production functions and perfect factor markets, however, do not yield any heterogeneity in the production sector despite monopolistic competition.

There are three different ways to model agent heterogeneity. As CASTANEDA et al. (2003) notes, models with identical utility functions across households have in general problems to achieve a realistic income distribution. This may be the reason why PALIVOS (2004) and KAPLAN et al. (2016) allow two different types of households. Like it was mentioned in the previous section, PALIVOS (2004) designs altruistic and egoistic households, the former care about their descendants, the latter do not. WILLIAMSON (2008) makes it random whether households prefer the goods exchange with another group of households or whether they prefer trading within their group. KAPLAN et al. (2016), in contrast, varies the level of impatience of households. MEH et al. (2008) sets different parameters in the utility function that has yet the same shape for all population classes.

As an alternative approach to model agent heterogeneity, ex ante identical households can experience stochastic shocks to their capital or skill endowment (JIN (2009), JIN (2010), CASTANEDA et al. (2003)). This allows to derive a single decision rule for all agents and turns an arbitrarily determined split of the population unnecessary. Those stochastic shock can either occur once at the "birth" of an agent and hold on (JIN, 2009). Or the households are exposed to random shocks at every period. Both variants have in common that every agent has the same policy rule due to identical preferences, however, the different endowment levels they start from leads to cross-sectional dispersion. In the first case, the non-trivial intial distribution carries on over time whereas in the second, the ongoing random shocks influence the cross-sectional distribution, too. Continued endowment shocks are mostly modeled for the skill endowment at period t, s_t, in form of a first-order Markov chain,

$$P(s_{t+1}|s_t) = \Gamma(s_{t+1}, s_t), \tag{4.1}$$

P. Dörr, *The Impact of Monetary Policy on Economic Inequality*,
BestMasters, https://doi.org/10.1007/978-3-658-24835-2_4

(CASTANEDA et al. (2003), LEE (2010), KAPLAN et al. (2016)). Markov chains have a stable distribution in the long run, hence the share of each attainable skill-level converges, though, this is in general numerically computed. A simple implementation of continued endowment shocks would be the separation between employed and unemployed households, meaning that there are only two possible states, $s \in \mathscr{S}, |\mathscr{S}| = 2$ (HEER and MAUSSNER, 2009, chap. 7). Note that this approach is only possible in a discrete time and skill-level setting. A continuous skill endowment, in contract, is used in JIN (2010). There, the skill level growth underlies an investment decision of the agent who optimizes his continuously timed utility.

Randomness at the micro-level often cancels out at the aggregate level such that in sum, there is no aggregate uncertainty (e.g. in HEER and MAUSSNER (2009, chap. 7) and WILLIAMSON (2008)). Alternatively, macroeconomic shocks can be included, too, (e.g. in the prodcution technology) leading to an aggregate risk.

The works of KAPLAN et al. (2016) and WILLIAMSON (2008) combine both channels to design heterogeneity, the latter associates macroeconomic risk with the money growth rule. However, for a one period shock in money supply, WILLIAMSON (2008) shows that the change in the share of money holdings of financial market (dis-)connected population groups vanishes over time.

Like it was mentioned in section 2, another option is to modify the level of risk aversion in a model without perfect foresight. While risk-neutral agents may invest their money in financial assets whose return cancel out inflation in expectation, risk-averse agents may rather hold cash and are thus subject to inflation. Then, inflation would have a distributional effect, too. However, this aspect will not be considered further in the theoretical part of this thesis. It is mentioned in several empirical papers, though (e.g. KANE and MORISETT (1993), EASTERLY and FISCHER (2001)).
A last way to model heterogeneity is the use of OG models. The age of household varies and thus their chance to have accumulated capital, especially when they face endowment shocks like in equation (4.1) (HUGGETT, 1996). The capital accumulation then would be higher for ex ante identical households who were lucky to experience relatively few/short unemployment/income spells. Additionally, the preferences may differ along the life span of agents (PALIVOS, 2004).

Note that papers that derive an analytical solution for the interaction between monetary policy and the income distribution (e.g. LONGARETTI et al. (2006), JIN (2009), JIN (2010)) only use the distribution's second moment for computability reasons. However, the income distribution (and especially wealth) is (highly) skewed (CASTANEDA et al., 2003), which can be expressed by the third moment if a distribution has moments. The alterantive to this limitation to the second moment, though, would be a numerical solution to an equilibrium distribution on the computer (HEER and MAUSSNER, 2009, chap. 7) or Monte-Carlo Simulation. This happens in the framework of DSGEs. Such derivations of the income distribution can be done via discretization of the continuous variable. Consequently, there is a trade-off between the exactitude of the computation and the tractability, not only between analytical and numerical approaches, but even within the numerical approaches. Nevertheless, in the empirical research, inequality measures that take skewness into account should be employed in order to capture this feature of the income distribution.

This section has focused on theoretical models that are analytically tractable. However, the tractability is paid with reduced complexity in the set-up. On the other hand, for numerically solved models, it remains unclear whether both, the qualitative and quantitative conclusions result from either the model mechanisms or the specific parameter vector chosen.

5 Combining General Equilibrium Models and Agent Heterogeneity

5.1 Model Set-up

It becomes clear from the previous sections that there are several possbilities to combine general equilibrium models with agent heterogeneity. Additionally, one can choose between a multitude of monetary policy measures and rules and the ways to connect them to the economy's real sphere.

The approach of JIN (2010) has the appealing features that it includes two economic sectors, has two different income channels - assets and labor - and allows to endogenously accumulate human capital. No a priori differentiation between economic agents is employed, neither in the shape of preferences nor in the parameter setting in the utility function. As those differentiations often have a slight taste of arbitrariness, this a further argument for ex ante identical economic agents. The analytical expression for the composition of income variance is appropriate for the analysis of monetary policy shocks. The ambiguous effect of monetary policy depending on the distribution of human and financial capital would be a possible explanation for the arguable empirical evidence. Finally, JIN (2010) does not employ price stickiness which is an arguable assumption, too, because the quantitative effect is small and the money transmission process remains unclear (WILLIAMSON, 2008). Furthermore, there is often no argument given why firms need to stick to price for an average period of length $\frac{1}{\theta}$ (cf. section 3). So I will focus on a model similar to JIN (2010) and its predecessors (JIN (2009), GARCÍA-PEÑALOSA and TURNOVSKY (2006)). However, admittedly, the money transmission process is undefined in those models, too.

This means that the introduced model is within the framework of endogenous growth. The economy consists of a continuum of infinitely lived households $h \in [0,1]$ that can either invest, hold money or consume a single good c. However, the production side of the economy consists of two sectors of which one builds the investment good Y_1 while the other supplies the consumption good, $Y_2 = C$. Firms in both sectors employ a Cobb-Douglas type production function,

$$Y_j = A_j K_j^{\alpha_j} L_j^{1-\alpha_j}, \qquad j \in \{1,2\} \tag{5.1}$$

and behave competitively on the goods and factor markets. This leads to the following factor demand functions:

$$L_j = (1-\alpha_j)\frac{Y_j}{w_j} \tag{5.2}$$

P. Dörr, *The Impact of Monetary Policy on Economic Inequality*,
BestMasters, https://doi.org/10.1007/978-3-658-24835-2_5

$$K_j = \alpha_j \frac{Y_j}{i}. \tag{5.3}$$

In the following, I will ignore capital depreciation, which is also implicitly found in the capital demand function (5.3): There is no depreciation rate in the function. Note that technology A_1 has an important role in the model, although it does not re-appear in the following: With $A_1 = 1$, plugging (5.2) and (5.3) into (5.1) would lead to $i = \alpha_1^{\alpha_1}(1-\alpha_1)^{1-\alpha_1} < 1$ which is contrary to a positive annual interest rate.

The households, on the other hand, are differently endowed with initial capital $a_h(0)$, cash $m_h(0)$ and skill $s_h(0)$, but can invest in both capital types. Human capital investment is a time investment of efficiency labor units e_h:

$$\dot{s}_h = f(e_h)$$

The household can only decide between time investment and labor; the labor supply is inelastic otherwise.

Time subscripts are omitted as a continuous time framework is employed, i.e. actually $c_h = c_h(t)$ etc. In order to guarantee skill accumulation and hence endogenous growth, it is sufficient that a growth of s_h increases labor income, too, as will be shown in the subsequent. Alternatively, the utility function could include some valuation of education/skill. Agents underly a CIA, i.e. consumption must be paid from nominal money holdings m_h, but in contrast to JIN (2009) and JIN (2010), nominal constraints are set. This returns the following optimization problem:

$$\max \int_0^\infty \exp(-\rho t) u(c_h, s_h) \mathrm{d}t \qquad \text{s.t.} \tag{5.4}$$

$$Pc_h + \dot{a}_h + \dot{m}_h = w_j(s_h - e_h) + ia_h + m_h \tag{5.5}$$

$$Pc_h = m_h, \tag{5.6}$$

$$\dot{s}_h = f(e_h), \tag{5.7}$$

where w_j is the nominal wage in economic sector j and i represents the instantaneous nominal interest. Equation (5.5) is a typical Budget Constraint (BC): Households earn or hold what is on the right hand side and can use it either to consume, save or accumulate cash. Additionally, note that household cannot borrow under (5.5), but can desave: A priori, there is no restriction that $\dot{a}_h \geq 0$. Taking $\imath$ as the annual interest rate, i follows from $\lim_{n\to\infty}\left(1+\frac{\imath}{n}\right)^n = \exp(\imath) =: i$. Subscript j on w is used to discuss later on labor market frictions. As will be shown in the next section, labor market segmentation that returns diverging wages w_1 and w_2 do not have an impact on the BGP as long as both wages grow by the same rate. However, the mechanisms that lead to labor market segmentation are not designed. DEMEKAS (1990) assumes one sectoral wage to be rigid above the equilibrium - this rigidity would need to be relaxed in the introduced model. One possible reason for an above equilibrium wage could be e.q. bargaining power of trade unions.

In its general formulation, the posed optimizatin problem allows the individual utility to depend on the skill-level, too. Further research therefore may expand the introduced model to an economy that values education per se. This, however, possibly makes the individual skill accumulation a nonlinear function of time investment and one would need to reinvestigate solvability. Later on, skill level will be ignored in the utility. The Lagrangian is thus, taking integrals by part (WÄLDE, 2011),

$$\mathscr{L} = \int_0^\infty \exp(-\rho t)u(c_h, s_h) + \tilde{\lambda}\left(w_j(s_h - e_h) + ia_h + m_h - Pc_h\right) + \tilde{\mu} f(e_h) \\ + \tilde{\eta}(m_h - Pc_h) + \dot{\tilde{\lambda}}\left(a_h + m_h\right) + \dot{\tilde{\mu}} s_h \mathrm{d}t, \quad (5.8)$$

yielding the following first order conditions:

$$\frac{\partial \mathscr{L}}{\partial c_h} = u'_c(c_h, s_h) - \lambda P - \eta P \stackrel{!}{=} 0 \quad (5.9)$$

$$\frac{\partial \mathscr{L}}{\partial e_h} = -\lambda w_j + \mu f' \stackrel{!}{=} 0 \quad (5.10)$$

$$\frac{\partial \mathscr{L}}{\partial s_h} = u'_s(c_h, s_h) + \lambda w_j + \dot{\mu} - \rho\mu \stackrel{!}{=} 0 \quad (5.11)$$

$$\frac{\partial \mathscr{L}}{\partial a_h} = i\lambda + \dot{\lambda} - \rho\lambda \stackrel{!}{=} 0 \quad (5.12)$$

$$\frac{\partial \mathscr{L}}{\partial m_h} = \lambda + \eta + \dot{\lambda} - \rho\lambda \stackrel{!}{=} 0, \quad (5.13)$$

where $\lambda = \exp(-\rho t)\tilde{\lambda}$ etc. and the multipliers are individual specific, i.e. $\lambda = \lambda_h$. Additionally, the classical no-Ponzi game conditions,

$$\lim_{t\to\infty} \exp(-\rho t)\tilde{\lambda}_h(t)a_h(t) = 0, \quad (5.14)$$

$$\lim_{t\to\infty} \exp(-\rho t)\tilde{\lambda}_h(t)m_h(t) = 0, \quad (5.15)$$

$$\lim_{t\to\infty} \exp(-\rho t)\tilde{\mu}_h(t)s_h(t) = 0, \quad (5.16)$$

must hold. For the sake of simplicity and solvability, I assume the following family of utility functions:

$$u(c_h, s_h) = \frac{c_h^{1-\sigma} - 1}{1-\sigma}, \qquad \sigma > 0, \quad (5.17)$$

where the case $\sigma = 1$ stands for a logarithmic utility. This means that overall utility would be time-separable in the discrete time case. In addition, the utility function has a constant Intertemporal Elasticity of Substitution (IES), $\frac{1}{\sigma}$, as can easily be verified:

$$
\begin{aligned}
&-\lim_{\Delta\to 0} \frac{c_h(t)}{c_h(t+\Delta)} \cdot \frac{u'(c_h(t+\Delta))}{u'(c_h(t))} \cdot \frac{\mathrm{d}\left(\frac{c_h(t+\Delta)}{c_h(t)}\right)}{\mathrm{d}\left(\frac{u'(c_h(t+\Delta))}{u'(c_h(t))}\right)} \\
&= -\frac{1}{\frac{\dot{c}_h}{c_h}} \cdot \left(\frac{\dot{c}_h}{c_h}\right)^{-\sigma} \cdot \frac{\mathrm{d}\left(\frac{\dot{c}_h}{c_h}\right)}{\mathrm{d}\left(\left(\frac{\dot{c}_h}{c_h}\right)^{-\sigma}\right)} \\
&= -x^{\frac{1}{\sigma}} \cdot x \cdot \frac{\mathrm{d}x^{\frac{-1}{\sigma}}}{\mathrm{d}x} = \frac{1}{\sigma}, \qquad \left(x := \left(\frac{\dot{c}_h}{c_h}\right)^{-\sigma}\right),
\end{aligned}
$$

meaning that marginal instantaneous utility decreases by $\frac{1}{\sigma}$ when consumption is marginally temporarily delayed. Usually, this delay is due to the substitution effect when interest rates increase: Households get more return on their savings, hence it is more attractive than current consumption. The skill accumulation function is assumed to be linear in e_h,

$$\dot{s}_h = \delta e_h. \tag{5.18}$$

Note that function (5.18) is already a generalization of JIN (2010) where $\delta = 1$. This generalization induces different conclusions but goes along with other differences between the introduced model and JIN (2010). For example, here, the second sector is an investment good sector whereas in JIN (2010), it is the education sector.
To anticipate the next section, the condition for a general equilibrium, market clearing, is

$$\int_0^1 s_h - e_h \mathrm{d}h = L = L_1 + L_2 \tag{5.19}$$

$$\int_0^1 a_h \mathrm{d}h = K = K_1 + K_2 = Y_1 \tag{5.20}$$

$$\int_0^1 c_h \mathrm{d}h = C = Y_2. \tag{5.21}$$

The market clearing condition (5.20) together with the production function (5.1) of sector 1 might appear as some sort of circular reasoning. However, the interpretation of the condition $K = K_1 + K_2 = A_1 K_1{}^{\alpha_1} L_1{}^{1-\alpha_1}$ is that production sector 1 has the role to actively preserve capital endowment. Figure (5.1) illustrates this relationship: At $t = 0$, take capital endowments K_1 and K_2 as given. These are used to produce (the consumption good C and) the investment good K, which is demanded by households that wish to save. Instantaneously (as $t \in \mathbb{R}_0^+$), the production of K is again splitted up into K_1 and K_2 in order to serve as input factors. This circularity of capital will prove to be essential for the equilibrium solution of the model.

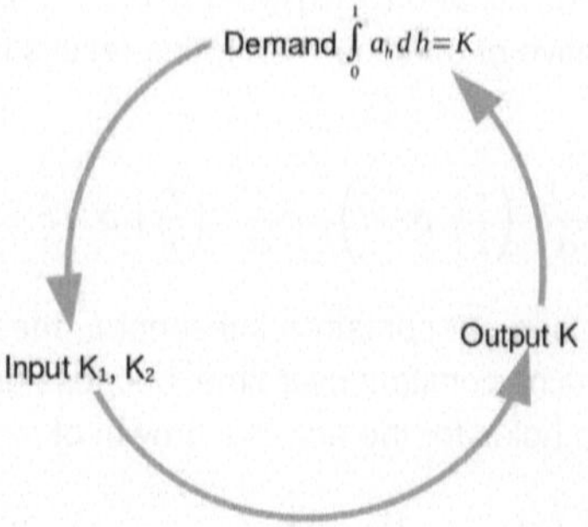

Figure 5.1: Relationship between Sector 1 Production and Capital Accumulation

Finally, and in accordance with JIN (2009), the monetary authority follows

$$\frac{\dot{M}}{M} = g + \pi \tag{5.22}$$

as monetary policy rule, i.e. nominal money growth equals the real money demand growth g plus the inflation rate. Consequently, the other nominal prices change according to

$$\frac{\dot{w}}{w} = \frac{\dot{\omega}}{\omega} + \pi \tag{5.23}$$

$$\frac{\dot{P}}{P} = \frac{\dot{p}}{p} + \pi, \tag{5.24}$$

that is real price change plus inflation, and the nominal interest equals the real one plus inflation, cf. equation (2.2). It is clear that real money demand growth is based on real income growth that is splitted into savings and consumption: For the latter, the CIA is binding, and therefore, (quantitative) consumption growth (and a possible change in real prices) directly translate to *real* money growth. As σ in (5.17) is strictly positive, the IES, $\frac{1}{\sigma}$, is finite and therefore, additional income is non-trivially split between both options. Finally, note that the IES should not be confused with the variance of income (components) $\sigma_\cdot^2$ that will be introduced later in order to have an analytically tractable measure of inequality.

5.2 Equilibrium - The Balanced Growth Path

The necessary conditions (5.12) and (5.13) yield $\eta = -(1-i)\lambda$ and $\dot{\lambda} = (\rho - i)\lambda$. Together with the time derivative of condition (5.9), this results in the following balanced growth of consumption:

$$\frac{\dot{c}_h}{c_h} = \frac{-1}{\sigma} \cdot \left(\frac{\dot{i}}{i} + \rho - i\right) = \frac{-1}{\sigma} \cdot \left(\frac{\dot{r}}{r} + \rho - r - \pi\right). \tag{5.25}$$

Note that the expression does not contain a subscript h, meaning that a household's consumption share $\varkappa_h^c$ remains constant over time, because growth rates are identical. Due to CIA (5.6), the same holds for the nominal growth of money demand,

$$\frac{\dot{m}_h}{m_h} = \frac{-1}{\sigma} \cdot \left(\frac{\dot{i}}{i} + \rho - i\right) + \frac{\dot{P}}{P} = \frac{-1}{\sigma} \cdot \left(\frac{\dot{r}}{r} + \rho - r\right) + \frac{\dot{p}}{p} + \frac{\sigma+1}{\sigma} \cdot \pi, \tag{5.26}$$

i.e. the growing demand in nominal money is due to both, real growth in c_h, therefore possibly changed real prices and inflation. The constant rate of growth of individual consumption leads to a constant aggregate growth rate of the same shape. The same applies to aggregate money demand because integrals are linear, $\int_0^1 q m_h \mathrm{d}h = q \int_0^1 m_h \mathrm{d}h = qM$, q being a constant. The growth in money demand must equal the growth in money supply, hence, under the policy rule (5.22),

$$\begin{aligned} g + \pi &= \frac{-1}{\sigma} \cdot \left(\frac{\dot{r}}{r} + \rho - r\right) + \frac{\dot{p}}{p} + \frac{\sigma+1}{\sigma} \cdot \pi, \qquad \Leftrightarrow \\ g &= \frac{-1}{\sigma} \cdot \left(\frac{\dot{r}}{r} + \rho - r - \pi\right) + \frac{\dot{p}}{p} = \frac{\dot{c}_h}{c_h} + \frac{\dot{p}}{p}, \end{aligned} \tag{5.27}$$

i.e. real money growth depends on consumption *quantity* growth and the change of value of consumption. However, note that equation (5.25) still contains inflation, indicating that money is non-neutral. This intermediate result is interesting as the growth rate is a first moment in the endogenous growth model and distributional aspects have not been discussed so far.

The result for consumption growth, equation (5.25), is standard for this type of consumption function (WÄLDE, 2011, chap 5.3.2). The higher the IES, i.e. the more current consumption reacts on a real interest rate change, the higher the growth rates of individual consumption and money demand under a given discount factor and interest rate: The IES determines the saving rate and therefore the wealth that can be consumed later on.

Obviously, g is an endogenous variable, thus, comparative statics concerning monetary policy is about π, which can be determined exongenously by the monetary authority, i.e. IT is a possible policy rule in the model. Later on, it will be shown that an equilibrium condition is $\pi = 0$.

From conditions (5.10) and (5.11), we learn that the BGP of the nominal wage must be

$$\frac{\dot{w}_j}{w_j} = i - \delta = r + \pi - \delta, \tag{5.28}$$

meaning that the marginal return of both income channels must equalize: The return of savings, i, equals the sum of return on educational investment δ and the general wage growth. Though the equation is derived from the factor supply (i.e. household) side, one could also argue from the factor demand side: When the interest rate increases, equality of marginal production costs requires that the other factor price, w_j, grows, too. However, parts of the additional income are known to be invested in education, reducing partially the labor demand, therefore the wage growth is less than i.

When there are market segmentations, however, wage equalization across industries $j \in \{1,2\}$ is inhibited. Nevertheless, the equilibrium only requires that both wages grow identically as can be seen in (5.28). Considering the growth of the model's state variables s_h and a_h, rewriting the constraints (5.18) and (5.5) yield

$$\frac{\dot{s}_h}{s_h} = \frac{\delta e_h}{s_h}, \tag{5.29}$$

$$\frac{\dot{a}_h}{a_h} = \frac{w_j(s_h - e_h)}{a_h} + r + \pi - \frac{\dot{m}_h}{m_h} \cdot \frac{m_h}{a_h}. \tag{5.30}$$

The second equation makes individual saving a function of the interest rate and two ratios, the ratio of labor income to wealth and the ratio of consumption and wealth ($Pc_h = m_h$). When both ratios remain constant, the saving rate remains constant under the BGP, too. As will be shown in the follwoing, on the BGP, the interest rate i and the real price p are constant and thus, the money growth rate is constant, too. Furthermore, one finds that the growth rates are not individual specific which is due to the fact that individuals only differ in their initial endowment, but not in their preferences or their access to information. Therefore they have the same decision rules.

Though it is not the topic of this thesis, note that solving (5.28) for δ and plugging the expression into (5.29) reveals a functional between wage growth, interest and the individual skill accumulation, $\frac{\dot{s}_h}{s_h} = \left(i - \frac{\dot{w}_j}{w_j}\right) \frac{e_h}{s_h}$. The first relation is negative because a growth of the return on "unskilled" labor implies less need to develop skills. The relation between interest and skill accumulation, however, is positive which might be due to the fact that a higher return on savings is an incentive to increase them. There are, however, two ways to do so: Either to consume less or to earn more. Those interdepencies could be analyzed in further research, however, table (A.1) in appendix A shows the correlation between average wage growth, the long term interest rate and the growth of the working age population share with tertiary education. Data come from 33 OECD countries from 2005 to 2014. Though more sophisticated empirical analysis would be indicated, the model predicts the signs in the correlation table. However, the correlation is low.

Turning to the production side, the growth of consumption makes factor demand increase in the consumption good producing sector:

$$\begin{aligned} \frac{\dot{L}_2}{L_2} &= \frac{\dot{C}}{C} - \frac{\dot{w}_2}{w_2} \\ &= \frac{-1}{\sigma}\cdot\left(\frac{\dot{i}}{i}+\rho\right) + \frac{\sigma+1}{\sigma}i+\delta = \frac{-1}{\sigma}\cdot\left(\frac{\dot{r}}{r}+\rho\right) + \frac{\sigma+1}{\sigma}\cdot r + \frac{\sigma+1}{\sigma}\cdot\pi+\delta \end{aligned} \tag{5.31}$$

$$\begin{aligned} \frac{\dot{K}_2}{K_2} &= \frac{\dot{C}}{C} - \frac{\dot{i}}{i} \\ &= \frac{-1}{\sigma}\cdot(\rho-i) + \frac{\sigma-1}{\sigma}\frac{\dot{i}}{i} = \frac{-1}{\sigma}\cdot(\rho-r-\pi) + \frac{\sigma-1}{\sigma}\cdot\frac{\dot{r}}{r}. \end{aligned} \tag{5.32}$$

Analogous time derivatives of equation (5.2) and (5.3) for industry 1 yield

$$\frac{\dot{L}_1}{L_1} = \frac{\dot{K}}{K} - \frac{\dot{w}_1}{w_1} \tag{5.33}$$

$$\frac{\dot{K}_1}{K_1} = \frac{\dot{K}}{K} - \frac{\dot{i}}{i}, \tag{5.34}$$

i.e. the market clearing condition for the factor market. These can be combined with the market clearing condition in the (investment) good market, which can be expressed as relative time derivative of equation (5.1). Realizing that wage growth equals (5.28), that the interest is competitive and that total capital growth is a weighted mean of the growth rates of capital in sector 1 and 2, one can combine the previous results to get

$$\frac{\dot{K}}{K} = \alpha_1\frac{\dot{K}_1}{K_1} + (1-\alpha_1)\frac{\dot{L}_1}{L_1} = \frac{\dot{K}_1}{K_1} - \frac{1-\alpha_1}{\alpha_1}(i-\delta) = \frac{\dot{K}_1}{K_1} - \frac{1-\alpha_1}{\alpha_1}(r+\pi-\delta). \tag{5.35}$$

This allows to equalize equation (5.32) and its pendant from sector 1, equation (5.34),

$$\frac{\dot{C}}{C} - \frac{\dot{K}_2}{K_2} = \frac{\dot{K}}{K} - \frac{\dot{K}_1}{K_1} \tag{5.36}$$

$$\frac{\dot{K}_2}{K_2} = \frac{\dot{C}}{C} + \frac{1-\alpha_1}{\alpha_1}(r+\pi-\delta), \tag{5.37}$$

which leads, combined with equation (5.32) to

$$\frac{\dot{i}}{i} = \frac{\dot{r}}{r} = \frac{1-\alpha_1}{\alpha_1}(\delta - r - \pi), \tag{5.38}$$

i.e. the interest rate evolves generically over time when $i \neq \delta$. This is due to the change in human capital s_h, which makes the relative price of input factors change because of the increased productivity of labor. The interdependency becomes clear as the parameter δ appears in the function: The higher the return of efficiency time investment in terms of future skill level, the higher the growth rate of the nominal interest rate. This can be explained with the positive crossed price elasticity of factor demand: The more human capital is employed, the more efficient is capital in the production, $\frac{\partial^2 Y_j}{\partial L_j \partial K_j} > 0$, leading to an increased capital demand, the latter raising the factor price. The parameter α_1 appears in the function because sector 1 supplies the economy with capital. Note that the change in the nominal interest rate results thus from a change in the real interest rate. From the capital demand function in sector 1 leading to equation (5.35), equation (5.37) and the fact that aggregate capital growth is a weighted sum, we can thus derive

$$\frac{\dot{K}_1}{K_1} = \frac{\dot{C}}{C} - \frac{\dot{r}}{r}\left(1 + \frac{K}{K_2}\right) \tag{5.39}$$

$$\frac{\dot{K}}{K} = \frac{\dot{C}}{C} - \frac{\dot{r}}{r} \cdot \frac{K}{K_2} = \frac{\dot{C}}{C} - \frac{r}{r-\alpha_1} \cdot \frac{\dot{r}}{r}. \tag{5.40}$$

This means that the average saving rate is at most as big as the consumption growth for positive interest rate growth. If so, reordering of (5.40) shows that the expansion in consumption then partially results from skill accumulation and the consequently augmented labor income because consumption growth is greater than aggregate saving.

The condition for the BGP, however, is that the ratio of relative (real) factor prices, $\frac{\omega}{r}$, remains constant:

$$\frac{\dot{\omega}}{\omega} = \frac{\dot{r}}{r}, \qquad i = \delta + \alpha_1 \pi \qquad \Leftrightarrow \tag{5.41}$$

$$r = \delta - (1-\alpha_1)\pi \qquad \Rightarrow \tag{5.42}$$

$$\frac{\dot{r}}{r} = -(1-\alpha_1)\pi \tag{5.43}$$

Thus, for non-negative inflation, capital accumulation is greater than or equal to consumption growth because the skill accumulation and hence augmented labor supply is not sufficient to compensate for the growing demand for consumption goods. Furthermore, one conclusion is that only a zero inflation policy may prevent the real wages and the real interest rate from a continuous decrease, i.e. money is non-neutral.

Though the continuous decrease of the real factor prices in the case of positive inflation is an unusual result, the outcome that money is non-neutral and that the economy grows at a constant rate are welcomed conclusions that allow to go on with the analysis.

Although this case is not considered here, it would be interesting to assume an exogenous growth of δ. Possibly, an exogeneous growth of δ would require the monetary authority to actively orientate its policy at the developments on the labor market. In the following, the BGP shall be considered and, once the economy has reached its equilibrium path, small deviations from the equilibrium and its impact on inequality.

To make individual and aggregate values grow, $\rho < i$ must hold, as can be seen from (5.25). Additionally, the continuous decrease of i clashes with the equilibrium interest rate. Thus, the only sensible monetary policy would be to keep price levels constant, i.e. $\pi = 0$, a very special IT policy. Then, all economic sectors grow at the same rate, establishing the BGP. This case shall be considered here.

Aggregate production value can be expressed as $Y = w_1 L_1 + w_2 L_2 + iK$ and the constant growth of both sectors, $\frac{\dot{K}}{K} = \frac{\dot{C}}{C}$ for $\delta = i$, imply that the factor shares of GDP remain constant over time, too. Nevertheless, this does not mean that income shares among agents remain unchanged. This has to be shown next.

5.3 Stability of the Income Distribution

Let $y_h = w_j(s_h - e_h) + ia_h$ denote household h's total income and $\varkappa_h^y = \frac{y_h}{Y}$ be the total income share. Like in JIN (2009) and JIN (2010), total income/wealth share can be expressed as a weighted mean of labor income share $\varkappa_h^w$ and share of capital endowment $\varkappa_h^a$

$$\varkappa_h^y = \phi \varkappa_h^a + (1 - \phi)\varkappa_h^w \tag{5.44}$$

$$\phi = \frac{iK}{Y} \tag{5.45}$$

On the BGP, $\dot{\phi} = 0$ because sector 1 and 2 grow with the same rate: As illustration take equation (5.40) with $\frac{\dot{r}}{r} = 0$. Hence their weighted sum, which must equal Y, grows at the same rate, too. The nominal interest rate remains constant (cf. equation (5.43) with

$\pi = 0$), too, under the BGP. The proof of the constancy of $\varkappa_h^a$ is similar to JIN (2009): The aggregate no-Ponzi scheme condition for capital accumulation is

$$\lim_{t\to\infty} \exp(-\rho t)\tilde{\lambda}(t)K(t) = 0 \quad \Leftrightarrow \quad \frac{\dot{\lambda}}{\lambda} + \frac{\dot{K}}{K} - \rho < 0 \tag{5.46}$$

$$\frac{\dot{K}}{K} < i. \tag{5.47}$$

This implies that labor in sector 1 and 2 must not grow faster than i neither because otherwise the composition of GDP between capital and labor income, $Y = iK + \bar{w}L$, would change. Due to the possibly different parameters α_1 and α_2 this would imply different growth rates across the economic sectors which is contrary to the results of the previous section. However, if the individual capital share was to change, it would have the shape

$$\dot{\varkappa}_h^a = \left(\frac{\dot{a}_h}{a_h} - \frac{\dot{K}}{K}\right)\varkappa_h^a > \left(\frac{\dot{a}_h}{a_h} - i\right)\varkappa_h^a. \tag{5.48}$$

From equation (5.30), we learn that $\left(\frac{\dot{a}_h}{a_h} - i\right) \geq 0$ because $\frac{\dot{a}_h}{a_h}$ must be non-negative per se for a stable equilibrium and due to the circularity of capital, cf. figure (5.1), it is greater than the interest. Nonetheless, the capital share's upper bound is 1, consequently there cannot be an unbounded growth as implied by the linear function (5.48). Therefore, the capital share cannot change over time on the BGP. Thus, if $\varkappa_h^w$ remains constant, too, then the total income share of individual h is constant on the BGP. This has to be shown next.

The analogous aggregate no-Ponzi condition to (5.46) for the production factor labor is

$$\frac{\dot{S}}{S} < \delta. \tag{5.49}$$

This condition is weaker than (5.46) as $\delta = i > \frac{\dot{K}}{K} = \frac{\dot{L}}{L} = \frac{\dot{S}}{S-E} > \frac{\dot{S}}{S}$, i.e. if the no-Ponzi condition (5.46) is fulfilled, the second condition holds, too.

In order to show the constancy of $\varkappa_h^w$, we exploit the BC corrected by the CIA. Dividing the adapted BC by GDP yields

$$\frac{\dot{a}_h + \dot{m}_h}{iK + \overline{w}L} = \frac{\overline{w}L}{iK + \overline{w}L}\varkappa_h^w + \frac{iK}{iK + \overline{w}L}\varkappa_h^a \quad \Leftrightarrow$$

$$\varkappa_h^w = \frac{\dot{a}_h + \dot{m}_h}{\overline{w}L} - \frac{iK}{\overline{w}L}\varkappa_h^a = \frac{\dot{a}_h}{a_h} \cdot \frac{K}{\overline{w}L} \cdot \varkappa_h^a + \frac{\dot{m}_h}{m_h} \cdot \frac{m_h}{\overline{w}L} - \frac{iK}{\overline{w}L}\varkappa_h^a, \tag{5.50}$$

where $\overline{w} = \frac{L_1}{L}\overline{w}_1 + \frac{L_2}{L}w_2$. Exploiting the fact that $\frac{\dot{a}_h}{a_h}$ and $\varkappa_h^a$ are constant over time and that $\frac{\dot{K}}{K} = \frac{\dot{L}}{L}$, one gets for the time derivative

$$\dot{\varkappa}_h^w = \frac{\dot{m}_h}{m_h} \cdot \left(\frac{\dot{m}_h}{\overline{w}L} - \frac{m_h}{\overline{w}L} \cdot \frac{\dot{L}}{L} \right).$$

However, using $\frac{\dot{L}}{L} = \frac{r+\pi-\rho-\frac{\dot{r}}{r}}{\sigma}$ and (5.26), this simplifies to

$$\begin{aligned}\dot{\varkappa}_h^w &= \frac{\dot{m}_h}{m_h} \cdot \frac{m_h}{\overline{w}L} \cdot \left(\frac{\dot{p}}{p} + \pi \right) \\ &= \left(\left(\frac{\dot{p}}{p} + \pi \right)^2 - \left(\frac{\dot{p}}{p} + \pi \right) \cdot \frac{1}{\sigma} \left(\frac{\dot{r}}{r} + \rho - r - \pi \right) \right) \cdot \frac{c_h}{w_j(s_h - e_h)} \varkappa_h^w. \end{aligned} \tag{5.51}$$

Under the stated assumptions, i.e. $\pi = 0$ (and consequently $\frac{\dot{r}}{r} = 0$) and $\rho < i = r + \pi$, the first term is non-negative. However, strict positivity would lead to the same contradiction like for capital share growth: When household h's share grows, then another household's share must decrease as the sum of shares is bounded to 1. Therefore, the labor income share of each household must be constant and the real price change of the consumption good, $\frac{\dot{p}}{p}$, equals 0 on the BGP.

However, this does not exclude marginal deviations from the BGP and a marginal impact on the income distribution. Then, it is interesting whether the economy is capable to return to its equilibrium or falls into a chaotic state. Deviations that induce a change in the control variables such as e_h, however, imply a change in (future) state variables, such as a_h, too. Therefore, the stability must be accounted for in the whole economy.

Next, we consider the income distribution's second moment as a measure of inequality. Like it is easily computed and pointed out in JIN (2009), the mean and totals of $\varkappa_h^y$ and the other income shares equal 1 because the continuum of households lies in the unit interval. Hence the second moment equals

$$\sigma_y^2 = \int_0^1 (\varkappa_h^y)^2 \mathrm{d}h - 1 \qquad \Leftrightarrow \tag{5.52}$$

$$\begin{aligned}\sigma_y^2 &= \int_0^1 \phi^2 (\varkappa_h^a)^2 + 2\phi(1-\phi)\varkappa_h^a \varkappa_h^w + (1-\phi)^2 (\varkappa_h^w)^2 \mathrm{d}h - 1 \\ &= \phi^2 \sigma_a^2 + (1-\phi)^2 \sigma_w^2 + 2\phi(1-\phi)\sigma_{a,w} + 2\phi(1-\phi),\end{aligned} \tag{5.53}$$

where $\sigma_{a,w}$ denotes the covariance of the labor and capital income share. Note that all households follow the same policy rule and therefore the dispersion parameters - σ_a^2 and σ_w^2 - are constant along the BGP and determined by the initial distribution of $s_h(0)$ and $a_h(0)$. This, however, implies that the covariance $\sigma_{a,w}$ is also solely influenced by the initial common distribution of those two state variables. This is the reason why JIN

(2009) can assume that $\sigma_{a,w} = 0$ to ease the analysis.

5.4 Monetary Policy and Inequality

5.4.1 The Impact of a Nominal Interest Rate Change

As it is shown in the previous section, the income distribution remains constant over time along the BGP. However, there can be disturbances that make the economy deviate slightly from the BGP. Such disturbances could be induced by monetary policy, e.g. policy adjustment errors like they are implied in empirical analysis by the use of regression residuals (ROMER and ROMER (2004), COIBION et al. (2012)). Thus, either the price level or the nominal inflation rate or both are altered. These scenarios shall be analyzed in this section.

The main objective of this section is to analyze $\frac{\mathrm{d}\sigma_y^2}{\mathrm{d}i}$ and $\frac{\mathrm{d}\sigma_y^2}{\mathrm{d}\pi}$. As $i = r + \pi$, a change in i is equivalent to a change in the inflation rate: The real interest rate is an endogenous variable and therefore determined by the equation system whereas the inflation rate is an exogenous parameter which I set above conveniently to 0 in order to get a time-stable BGP.

In order to simplify the analysis, the envelope theorem must be employed: Briefly, the production factors $K(i,w)$ and $L(i,w)$ are the result of an optimization problem given factor prices, and the subsequent algebra does not require a re-derivation of those variables with respect to i (nor w if it was considered). This helps e.g. when taking the derivative $\frac{\mathrm{d}\phi}{\mathrm{d}i}$. The envelope theorem is also important when considering that a_h and s_h are already the outcomes of earlier optimization problems, i.e. optimal decision rules, and thus need not be re-analyzed after a contamporaneous interest or inflation rate change, $\mathrm{d}i$ or $\mathrm{d}\pi$. Thus, in a very general manner, we can write

$$\begin{aligned}\frac{\mathrm{d}\sigma_y^2}{\mathrm{d}i} &= 2\phi\frac{K}{Y}\sigma_a^2 + \phi^2\frac{\mathrm{d}\sigma_a^2}{\mathrm{d}i} - 2(1-\phi)\frac{K}{Y}\sigma_w^2 + (1-\phi)^2\frac{\mathrm{d}\sigma_w^2}{\mathrm{d}i} + \\ &\quad 2(1-2\phi)\frac{K}{Y}\sigma_{a,w} + 2(\phi-\phi^2)\frac{\mathrm{d}\sigma_{a,w}}{\mathrm{d}i} \\ &= 2\frac{K}{Y}\left(\phi\sigma_a^2 - (1-\phi)\sigma_w^2 + (1-2\phi)\sigma_{a,w}\right) + \\ &\quad \left(\phi^2\frac{\mathrm{d}\sigma_a^2}{\mathrm{d}i} + (1-\phi)^2\frac{\mathrm{d}\sigma_w^2}{\mathrm{d}i} + 2(\phi-\phi^2)\frac{\mathrm{d}\sigma_{a,w}}{\mathrm{d}i}\right). \end{aligned} \tag{5.54}$$

As $\phi = \frac{iK}{Y}$, and neither K nor L require a derivation with respect to i, the weighting factor remains unchanged. JIN (2009) considers the variance σ_a^2 fix along the BGP and does not include the development of human capital, because skill is modelled as innate and unchangeable endowment. Therefore, $\frac{\mathrm{d}\sigma_a^2}{\mathrm{d}i}$ and $\frac{\mathrm{d}\sigma_w^2}{\mathrm{d}i}$ equal 0 in the cited paper and furthermore, the covariance term is assumed to be zero. Later on it will be proved that the dispersion of the income components does not react to a nominal interest rate change neither in our model. However, for the time being, this is a possibility that must be considered in the calculus. Another argument for the necessity of an deeper insight to $\frac{\mathrm{d}\sigma_{\cdot}^2}{\mathrm{d}i}$ is that JIN (2009) analyzes the impact on inequality of nominal money growth rather than a change in the inflation and consequently in the nominal interest rate.

Nevertheless, nominal money growth goes along with a (transitory) increase in the inflation rate and thus in the nominal interest, cf. equation (2.2). Hence, the result of the introduced model will prove to be similar to JIN (2009): An increase or decrease on income inequality following a monetary policy measure has a priori ambiguous sign and depends on the composition of total income inequality. When skill/labor heterogeneity dominates capital heterogeneity in a certain manner, then an increase in the interest rate reduces inequality. However, this result is only admissible when several terms equal 0 in equation (5.54). For a deeper analysis, the following derivatives are of special interest:

$$\frac{\mathrm{d}\varkappa_h^y}{\mathrm{d}i} = \frac{K}{Y}\varkappa_h^a + \phi\frac{\mathrm{d}\varkappa_h^a}{\mathrm{d}i} - \frac{K}{Y}\varkappa_h^w + (1-\phi)\frac{\mathrm{d}\varkappa_h^w}{\mathrm{d}i} \tag{5.55}$$

$$\frac{\mathrm{d}\varkappa_h^y}{\mathrm{d}\pi} = \phi\frac{\mathrm{d}\varkappa_h^a}{\mathrm{d}\pi} + (1-\phi)\frac{\mathrm{d}\varkappa_h^w}{\mathrm{d}\pi}. \tag{5.56}$$

I focus simultaneously on the impact of inflation and of a nominal interest rate change because the inflation rate π mostly appears in the previous equations through its relation to i: $\frac{\mathrm{d}i}{\mathrm{d}\pi} = \alpha_1$, cf. equation (5.41). For an analysis of the effect of an inflation rate change from $\pi = 0$ to $\mathrm{d}\pi$, only the additional impact on the nominal wage rate and the nominal consumption price must be added. These derivatives are important because the integral is finite and under the differentiability of (5.55), one can use the Leibniz integration rule, $\frac{\mathrm{d}\sigma_y^2}{\mathrm{d}i} = \frac{\mathrm{d}\int_0^1 (\varkappa_h^y)^2 \mathrm{d}h}{\mathrm{d}i} = \frac{\int_0^1 2\varkappa_h^y (\varkappa_h^y)_i' \mathrm{d}h}{\mathrm{d}i}$.

In order to make a statement about the sign of the derivatives, one must take into account several influence factors. For example, the nominal interest rate growth changes:

$$\mathrm{d}\frac{\dot{i}}{i} = -\frac{1-\alpha_1}{\alpha_1}\mathrm{d}i < 0, \tag{5.57}$$

meaning that the interest rate will decrease over time after an instantaneous positive change of i, $\mathrm{d}i > 0$. Taking into consideration that the original growth rate is 0, this leads to a newly induced interest change rate of the size $\frac{\dot{i}'}{i'} = 0 + \mathrm{d}\frac{\dot{i}}{i} = -\frac{1-\alpha_1}{\alpha_1}$, meaning that the interest rate will re-adjust after the shock, because once the rate has re-achieved the original level of i, $\delta = i$ holds once again and there will be zero growth in i. The higher the capital intensity in the investment sector, i.e. the closer α_1 is to 1, the slower the return to the original interest rate level because the slower the sector adapts to the change in the individual saving decision: The income effect makes individuals save less when the interest rate is higher. Thus, less capital is demanded from producers in sector 1. Nevertheless, the impact on the demand for capital as input factor, K_1, is lower when the general capital intensity in sector 1 is high, i.e. factor demand on K_1 remains at a relatively high level.

The transitory change in the interest rate, however, leads to the following (transitory) change in the individual consumption and money demand growth

$$\mathrm{d}\frac{\dot{c}_h}{c_h} = \mathrm{d}\frac{\dot{m}_h}{m_h} = \frac{1}{\sigma}\frac{1}{\alpha_1}\mathrm{d}i > 0. \tag{5.58}$$

While the direct impact of $\mathrm{d}i$ is negative (cf. equation (5.25) partially derived with respect to i), the transitory decrease in the interest rate (5.57) makes the consumption return to its original path. The speed of the re-adjustment depends obivously on the IES and interacts with the capital intensity of the investment sector for the reason given in the previous paragraph. Hence, the slower return to the BGP interest rate goes together with a slow return to the original consumption path.

Due to the CIA, these effects on consumption growth translate perfectly to the individual money demand. Note that this result would be different when analyizing the impact of $\mathrm{d}\pi$, because then, the nominal price level P would change, too, which has a larger impact on nominal money demand than on consumption quantity, cf. equation (5.25) and (5.26). In any case, the investment good sector serves as a multiplier. These derivations allow us to conclude with the equation on individual capital accumulation (5.30)

$$\mathrm{d}\frac{\dot{a}_h}{a_h} = \left(1 - \frac{1}{\sigma}\frac{1}{\alpha_1}\frac{m_h}{a_h}\right)\mathrm{d}i, \tag{5.59}$$

implying that the behaviour of capital accumulation will change. Again, the sign of that change depends again on the IES and the capital intensity of the investment sector.

There are two opposite effects on the saving behaviour whose relation determines the sign in (5.59). When the interest rate re-adjusts, i.e. i returns from its transitory high, the relative decrease makes saving less attractive (after an instantaneous boom due to $\mathrm{d}i > 0$). Therefore, the change in the consumption growth translates to the saving behaviour. However, this effect might be aggravated ($\frac{m_h}{a_h} > 1$) when a household already consumes relatively much or mildered when it holds already relatively many assets ($\frac{m_h}{a_h} < 1$). In the first situation, there is no (capital) income effect that could serve as counter-weight to the substitution effect of interest rate decrease, whereas in the second case, there is. This induces a transitory diverging saving behaviour amongst households, which will effect the capital income dispersion in the long run: When the interest rate has returned to its equilibrium level, households return to their overall growth rate $\frac{\dot{K}}{K}$, and consequently, the transitory effect will not be wiped out but establishes a new BGP asset dispersion level. Because the change in the interest rate makes households with relatively few assets save less and vice versa, the dispersion will increase capital income inequality, $\frac{\mathrm{d}\sigma_{\alpha}^2}{\mathrm{d}i} > 0$. This result is contrary to the statement in JIN (2009) that the capital income dispersion remains fixed after a change in nominal money growth. However, the different results may result from different model set-ups outlined in the previous subsections.

As long as the wage is unbounded (contrary to the case when e.g. market segmentation occurs), wage will grow over time after an increase in the nominal interest rate, $\mathrm{d}\frac{\dot{w}_j}{w_j} = di$, cf. equation (5.28). Note that this is in contrast to the development of the interest rate which is (transitorily) negative over time and only in a special case proportional to the original change in i (precisely, only if $\alpha_1 = 0.5$).

The time investment in education e_h, however, reacts (theoretically) on an interest rate change, too. Taking the total differential of equation (B.4) in appendix B with respect to i yields that the instantaneous investment in human capital remains unchanged after an increase in the interest rate. However, together with equation (B.6) it is revealed that

$$\frac{\dot{e}_h}{e_h} = \delta + \frac{i}{w_j}\frac{\dot{a}_h}{a_h}\frac{a_h}{e_h} \tag{5.60}$$

$$\mathrm{d}\frac{\dot{e}_h}{e_h} = \frac{a_h}{e_h}\left(\frac{i}{w_j}\left(1 - \frac{1}{\sigma}\frac{1}{\alpha_1}\frac{m_h}{a_h}\right) + \frac{1}{w_j}\frac{\dot{a}_h}{a_h}\right)\mathrm{d}i. \tag{5.61}$$

This expression is not equal for all households because the ratio $\frac{a_h}{e_h}$ depends on the intial distribution of $s_h(0)$ and $a_h(0)$ and therefore diverges across households even when they follow the same capital investment policy. Additionally, $\mathrm{d}\frac{\dot{a}_h}{a_h}$ varies among households, too, as discussed above. For the analysis in the next paragraph, note that equation (5.61) is linear in $\mathrm{d}\frac{\dot{a}_h}{a_h}$, i.e. it has the form $\mathrm{d}\frac{\dot{e}_h}{e_h} = \gamma_h + \beta_h \mathrm{d}\frac{\dot{a}_h}{a_h}$. Because $\gamma_h := \frac{a_h}{w_j e_h}\frac{\dot{a}_h}{a_h}\mathrm{d}i$, this parameter is household-specific but always non-negative. The same holds for $\beta_h := \frac{i a_h}{w_j e_h}$. Hence, the sign of $\mathrm{d}\frac{\dot{e}_h}{e_h}$ solely depends on the sign and amplitude of $\mathrm{d}\frac{\dot{a}_h}{a_h}$ and therefore the ratio between wealth a_h and consumption. If

$$\begin{aligned} i - \frac{1}{\sigma}\frac{1}{\alpha_1}\frac{m_h}{a_h}\cdot i + \frac{\dot{a}_h}{a_h} = i - \frac{1}{\sigma}\frac{1}{\alpha_1}\frac{m_h}{a_h}\cdot i + \frac{\dot{a}_h}{a_h} + \frac{1}{\sigma}(i - \rho) > 0 \quad &\Leftrightarrow \\ \alpha_1\left(\sigma + 1 - \frac{\rho}{i}\right) > \frac{m_h}{a_h}, & \end{aligned}$$

investment in human capital increases: Then, the successive return from $i_{BGP} + \mathrm{d}i$ back to i_{BGP} generates income losses of such importance that they must be compensated with higher labor income. This will mainly hold for households with large a_h, meaning the wealthy households, leading those households not only to accumulate additional capital more than average, but also to improve their situation on the labor market relatively to the unfavored.

The nominal wage rate, however, increases over time after an increase of i, as can be seen from equation (5.28), at least when there are market forces at place. However, this change applies to all agents. Therefore, I am not able to verify that the dispersion in labor income σ_w^2 remains constant. Rather than being constant, we observe that relatively wealthy households ($\frac{m_h}{a_h}$ close to 0) who increase their savings, too, tend to either increase their human capital or to decrease it less than poorer households. Therefore, the change of the individual income shares, $\varkappa_h^a$ and $\varkappa_h^w$ will tend into the same direction for a wealthy household h, but may differ from the behaviour of another household m. Hence, $\frac{\mathrm{d}(\varkappa_h^a \varkappa_h^w)}{\mathrm{d}i} = \varkappa_h^w \frac{\mathrm{d}\varkappa_h^a}{\mathrm{d}i} + \varkappa_h^a \frac{\mathrm{d}\varkappa_h^w}{\mathrm{d}i}$ will move into the same direction like the derivatives of the two factors when both have the same sign (note the positive intercept γ_h in the previous paragraph). Therefore, denoting by "$'$" the transitory, new values, e.g. $\varkappa_h^{a\prime} = \varkappa_h^a + \mathrm{d}\varkappa_h^a$, the new covariance becomes

$$\sigma'_{a,w} = \int_0^1 \varkappa_h^{a\prime} \varkappa_h^{w\prime} \mathrm{d}h - 1 \tag{5.62}$$

$$= \int_0^1 \varkappa_h^a \varkappa_h^w + \varkappa_h^a \mathrm{d}\varkappa_h^w + \varkappa_h^w \mathrm{d}\varkappa_h^a + \mathrm{d}\varkappa_h^w \mathrm{d}\varkappa_h^a \, \mathrm{d}h - 1$$

$$= \sigma_{a,w} + \int_0^1 \mathrm{d}(\varkappa_h^a \varkappa_h^w) + \mathrm{d}\varkappa_h^w \mathrm{d}\varkappa_h^a \, \mathrm{d}h$$

$$\neq \sigma_{a,w}. \tag{5.63}$$

Thus, even when the state variables were independently distributed initially, $\sigma_{a,w} = 0$, this is not generally the case after an interest rate change. Though the sign of $\frac{\mathrm{d}\sigma_{a,w}}{\mathrm{d}i}$ does not become clear from (5.62), it was noted earlier that rather those households who are wealthier tend to increase their human capital investment, too, the intuition says that $\sigma'_{a,w} > \sigma_{a,w}$.

Therefore, a clear-cut proposition like in JIN (2009) or JIN (2010) is not possible, but the dispersion of labor income would need to be very dominant in order to outweigh the impact of the capital income dispersion and the transitory dynamics (cf. the negative sign of $(1-\phi)\sigma_w^2$ in equation (5.54)).

One might argue that those transitory dynamics only correct the instantaneous income effects of an interest rate change, meaning that the non-zero valued $\mathrm{d}\sigma_{\cdot}^2$ are only adjustment after the instantaneous boom following $\mathrm{d}i$. Nevertheless, consider that a_h and s_h are already realized states at the time of the interest rate change and therefore their future values can be re-adjusted. This is why the dynamics must be analyzed in order to find out about the impact of an interest rate change. Although the transitory dynamics may be interpreted to balance instantaneous shifts in the control variables c_h and e_h, the pairs $\mathrm{d}\frac{\dot{c}_h}{c_h}$ and $\mathrm{d}c_h$ as well as $\mathrm{d}\frac{\dot{e}_h}{e_h}$ and $\mathrm{d}e_h$ will not cancel out each other. For example, the instantaneous shift of c_h does not even become clear neither from the BC and the CIA nor from the equilibrium analysis.

Next, we consider a change in the equilibrium inflation rate, $\pi = 0$. As mentioned above, the inflation rate intervenes in the model via its impact on the nominal interest rate i, $\mathrm{d}i = \alpha_1 \mathrm{d}\pi$. Therefore, an increase in the inflation rate from 0 to $\mathrm{d}\pi$ does not translate identically to the nominal interest rate. This is due to the non-neutrality of money outlined in the previous section; a shift in the price level creates an incentive to consume more at the present like the same amplitude change of the nominal interest rate. However, a shift in the inflation rate generates an intertemporal income effect even for those households that are rarely affected by a direct interest rate shift, i.e. those who mainly cover their consumption by labor income. The income effect makes such worker-households save, too; the increased saving makes the real interest rate decrease (cf. equation (5.42)) and thus moderates the nominal interest rate change to $\alpha_1 \mathrm{d}\pi$. The weaker reaction of wealthy households makes the interest rate raise less. Nevertheless, the analysis above can be transferred to a shift of the inflation rate. Simply plug in $\alpha_1 \mathrm{d}\pi$ instead of $\mathrm{d}i$.

5.4.2 Stability of the Balanced Growth Path

In this section, I turn to the question whether the economy will return to its BGP after a perturbation like a once-in-a-time positive inflation. As long as $\mathrm{d}\pi < \frac{1}{1-\alpha_1}$, we learn from equation (5.43) that $1 + \frac{\dot{r}}{r} \in (0,1)$ and thus, the interest rate will decrease to its original level geometrically and rather than diverge.

Figure (5.2) illustrates the stability of the BGP. The consumption behaviour is identical for all households and plotted in the graph. When $\mathrm{d}\pi < \frac{1}{1-\alpha_1}$ the change of the interest rate will be less than $\frac{\alpha_1}{1-\alpha_1}$, $\mathrm{d}i < \frac{\alpha_1}{1-\alpha_1}$. Thus, the deviance of the interest rate growth $\frac{\dot{i}}{i}$ from 0 is less than 1 in absolute terms. This reduces the (positive) wage growth rate iteratively, which again feeds back to the interest rate change due to the interdependeny of production factors and their prices. Note that due to $\mathrm{d}i > 0$ and $\mathrm{d}\frac{\dot{w}}{w} > 0$, household income is above the BGP level and therefore, one observes a positive shift in the consumption growth rate. The lower wage growth rates and the return to i_{BGP} following $\mathrm{d}\frac{\dot{i}}{i} < 0$ and consequently, the consumption growth rate finally reduces to its BGP level, too. The less the capital intensity in the investment good sector, i.e. the lower α_1, the wider the range of inflation shocks that allow the economy to return to its BGP because the less the circularity of capital that is illustrated in figure (5.1).

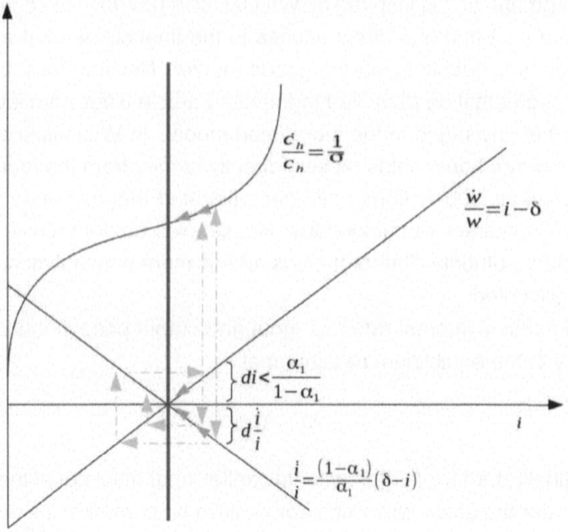

Figure 5.2: Stability of the BGP

Note that the fact that the consumption growth is above the equilibrium level comes from both the initial interest rate shock and the re-correction of the interest rate via $\frac{\dot{i}}{i}<0$. This does not mean that the control variable c_h might not suffer from an instantaneous decrease due to the intertemporal consumption substitution into the future after $\mathrm{d}i>0$. However, even if $\mathrm{d}c_h<0$ because the substitution effect outweighs the income effect, this means that more can be consumed in the future due to the higher return. As we consider a dynamic system, an optimal c_h is not apperent from the BC and the CIA because time is continuous and therefore, c_h changes immediately.

Finally, note that the real interest rate is endogenously determined in the model. Hence, the only way to increase the nominal interest rate is an increase in inflation, cf. equations (5.41) and, more generally, (2.2). As inflation is the consequence of nominal money growth, i.e. money growth that is not backed by the increased need of it due to qualitative and/or quantitative growth in consumption and investment, the deviations from the BGP analyzed here can be interpreted as expansionary monetary policy.

5.5 Labor Market Segmentation

Although the subscript j for the industry has been taken with, no special focus has lied so far on the role of labor market segmentation for the model. The idea to introduce market segmentation is inspired by WILLIAMSON (2008) who segments the model population into a part that has direct access to the financial market and another that policy measures only dribble to via the goods market. Nevertheless, the financial and goods market segmentation modelled in the cited article differ from labor market segmentation like it is envisaged in the introduced model. In WILLIAMSON (2008), only a part of the economy's households receive directly money from the monetary authority, whereas the previous subsections have demonstrated that monetary policy in the introduced model is indirect, but ubiquitous: Households do not receive additional cash from the monetary authority. Rather there is ad hoc more nominal money in the system that has to be allocated.

Having the nominal interest rate i as input and output price in the investment good sector, industry 1, the equiblirium requires that

$$K_1 = \alpha_1 K \tag{5.64}$$

because marginal return $i\alpha_1 \frac{K}{K_1}$ of additional capital input must equal the marginal costs of capital, i. Under the assumption of a competitive labor market, i.e. $w_1 = w_2 = w$, this results leads to

$$\frac{L_2}{L_1} = \frac{1-\alpha_2}{\alpha_2} \qquad \Leftrightarrow \qquad L1 = \alpha_2 L,$$

using equation (5.2). However, it is not necessary to equalize w_1 and w_2. Then, equations (5.64) and (5.2) lead to

$$\frac{w_2}{w_1} = \frac{\alpha_2}{1-\alpha_2} \cdot \frac{L_2}{L_1}, \tag{5.65}$$

which does not contradict the requirement of equal growth rates of L_1 and L_2. The circulary use of K as illsutrated in figure (5.1) allows to use both, the factor demand functions and the good demand function to determine the inter-sectoral allocation of K and consequently the equilibrium interest rate (5.41). This returns one degree of freedom in the model parameters because only three of the four factor demand functions (5.2) and (5.3) are needed. Hence, one equation is left that allows wage differentiation like in (5.65).

For example, assume $w_1 = \overline{w}_1$ fixed. Then,

$$\begin{aligned} L_1 &= (1-\alpha_1) \cdot K \cdot \frac{i}{\overline{w}_1} \\ L_2 &= L - L_1 \\ w_2 &= \overline{w}_1 \left(\frac{\overline{w}_1}{i} \frac{1}{1-\alpha_1} \frac{L}{K} - 1 \right). \end{aligned} \tag{5.66}$$

The second equation shows that there is a lower bound for the wage $\overline{w}_1$ such that the labor supply in sector 2 is positive,

$$\overline{w}_1 > (1-\alpha_1)\cdot i \cdot \frac{K}{L}.$$

In the following, let w denote the equilibrium wage under perfect labor market competition and let $\overline{w}_1 = \xi w,\ \xi > 1$. Where the segmentation shall not be further examined, an unspecificity that can also be found in DEMEKAS (1990). One possible reason for $\overline{w}_1 > w$ could be the unionization in industry 1 whereas sector 2 workers have no lobby. In contrast to the cited paper, the gap between competitive labor demand and segmented labor demand in sector 1 is not spelled in unemployment but absorbed by the second labor market, lowering the latter wage rate w_2.

For $1 < \xi < (1-\alpha_1)\frac{iK}{wL}$, $w < \overline{w}_1$ and $w_2 < w$. The allocation of agent h's labor force to either economic sector 1 or 2 is random, leading to $\mathrm{Cov}(\frac{w_j}{\overline{w}}, \frac{s_h - e_h}{L}) = 0$ where $\overline{w}$ is the average wage $\overline{w} = \frac{L_1}{L}\overline{w}_1 + \frac{L_2}{L}w_2$. Thus, knowing that $\mathrm{E}(\frac{w_j}{\overline{w}}) = \mathrm{E}(\frac{s_h - e_h}{L}) = 1$, the variance of the labor income share is

$$\begin{aligned}
\mathrm{Var}\left(\frac{w_j(s_h-e_h)}{\overline{w}L}\right) &= \mathrm{Var}\left(\frac{w_j}{\overline{w}}\right)\cdot \mathrm{Var}\left(\frac{s_h-e_h}{L}\right) + \mathrm{Var}\left(\frac{w_j}{\overline{w}}\right)\cdot \mathrm{E}\left(\left(\frac{s_h-e_h}{L}\right)^2\right) + \\
&\quad \mathrm{Var}\left(\frac{s_h-e_h}{L}\right)\cdot \mathrm{E}\left(\left(\frac{w_j}{\overline{w}}\right)^2\right) \\
&= 3\cdot \mathrm{Var}\left(\frac{w_j}{\overline{w}}\right)\cdot \mathrm{Var}\left(\frac{s_h-e_h}{L}\right) + \mathrm{Var}\left(\frac{w_j}{\overline{w}}\right) + \mathrm{Var}\left(\frac{s_h-e_h}{L}\right) \\
&> \mathrm{Var}\left(\frac{s_h-e_h}{L}\right),
\end{aligned}$$

where $\mathrm{Var}\left(\frac{s_h-e_h}{L}\right)$ is the variance of labor income share under a competitive labor market because then, the wage rate $w.$ cancels out. This means that labor market segmentation aggravates labor income dispersion and thus total income variation. This is due to the fact that in addition to the randomness of the initial allocation $s_h(0)$, there is now the instantaneous random assignment to one of the two labor markets where one is worse paid than the other. Note that despite the boundedness of $\overline{w}_1$, both wages must grow at the same rate in order to ensure the BGP when $i \neq \delta$.

When it comes to a deviation $\mathrm{d}i$ from the equilibrium interest rate $i = \delta$ as discussed in the previous subsection and there is labor market segmentation, then there is only one labor market (the "non-unionized" labor market) that is allowed to adjust the wage growth rate as function of $\mathrm{d}i$ if there is no wage indexation in the other market. Here, this would be the consumption good labor market. As we have learned from the previous subsection, the wage growth rate would increase in response to $\mathrm{d}i$ (cf. equation (5.28) and figure (5.2)). Additionally, $dw_2 > 0$ due to the positive cross-derivative $\frac{\partial^2 Y_2}{\partial K_2 \partial L_2} > 0$. Because $w_2 < w_1$, a nominal interest rate shock would thus reduce the difference between the two wage rates. Nevertheless, there are still transitory dynamics of human capital investment due to income effects and hence the direction of the labor income dispersion is even less clear-cut than in the subsection before. On the other hand, the transitory convergence of both wage rates - which happens when the bounded wage ($\overline{w}_1$) is not indexed - would counter-weigh the (probable) divergence of human capital accumulation as seen from equation (5.61).

Observing large labor market segmentations in reality, this model may reflect the ambiguity of the empirical evidence discussed in the subsequent section: Depending on the analyzed country and/or time interval, the one or the other of the discussed effects on labor income may overweigh.

6 Empirical Evidence

6.1 Previous Findings

The empirical evidence on the effect of monetary policy on economic inequality is ambiguous. There is not only a lack of clarity on whether it has an impact on the income and/or wealth distribution, and, if so, on which sign such an effect would have. But also the impact might be splitted into short- and long-run effects. Besides the effects that have been reflected in the introduced theoretical model of the previous section, there are also impact channels like household balance sheets, net debts and credits. Uncertainty about future inflation, which has not found its way into the endogenous growth model, may work on the income distribution, too.

One of the early empirical analysis is ROMER and ROMER (1998). The authors employ both, cross-sectional country data and longitudinal US data from 1969 to 1994. While the former serves to assess the long-run impact of inflation measured by the GDP deflator on the change of the head-count ratio poverty rate, the Gini coefficient and the income share of the lowest quintile of the income distribution, the use of the latter allows to elaborate a short-term, cyclical effect of inflation on poverty. As control variables, the authors use the change of the unemployment rate in the short-run analysis and (log-)GDP variability in the long-run. Simple OLS regressions are run. They find that expansionary monetary policy (i.e. a raise in inflation) lowers poverty in the short run but is harmful to the poors' income in the long run presumably because low inflation and demand variability stand for macroeconomic stability and other income boosting policy means. The argumentation of ROMER and ROMER (1998) about the positive short-term effect of expansionary monetary policy on inequality is similar to that in BIVENS (2015): Money growth can stabilize the economy in times of recession and thus save jobs. Unemployment, however, is an important (negative) income shock and therefore often leads to economic isolation.

The findings of EASTERLY and FISCHER (2001) are similar to ROMER and ROMER (1998): Using (mostly) cross-sectional country data, the authors find that inflation is positively related to poverty; however, the evidence for a significant relation between the lowest quintile's income share and inflation is ambiguous. On the other hand, the authors' main finding is about the perceived exposure to inflation: The (in several socio-economic dimensions) less privileged are more concerned about inflation than the better-off. As mentioned earlier, this may be due to their relative high proportion of cash holdings, which are not protected against/indexed to inflation.

The longitudinal analysis of ROMER and ROMER (1998) and thus their conclusions are based on US data, though. The highest inflation rate as measured by the Producer

P. Dörr, *The Impact of Monetary Policy on Economic Inequality*,
BestMasters, https://doi.org/10.1007/978-3-658-24835-2_6

Price Index (PPI) was 15.3% and 4.8% on average during their period of analysis[1]. Possibly it is the hyperinflation in Brazil during the period from 1970 to 1989 that leads KANE and MORISETT (1993) to a different result, although roughly the same time horizon is considered: Taking into account not only cash holdings, but also indexed assets and indexed wages, which only some parts of the income distribution have access to, the authors find that the hyperinflation period was regressive to the lower quintiles' total income share. This goes along with the perception in EASTERLY and FISCHER (2001). Here, it seems that the economic instability at that time outweighs any possibly positive effects of money expansion as found in ROMER and ROMER (1998). GDP growth is controlled for; the dependent variables are the average wages of the five income quintiles. However, data is annual and ranges from 1970 to 1989, giving a very low number of observations. The authors do not find any Phillips-curve like relation between inflation and unemployment neither, which could be due to the special economic situation of Brazil in that time period or due to the few observations.

Like the already mentioned papers, DAVTYAN (2016) uses inflation (in the US) as an indicator of monetary policy and finds that contractionary monetary policy reduces the Gini coefficient. Although the analysis is longitudinal, the qualitative result is the same like the cross-sectional analysis in ROMER and ROMER (1998). The latter interpret the cross-sectional result as a long-term relationship which would go along with the relatively long period of observation in DAVTYAN (2016), which is 1960 to 2012.

When inflation is considered to be expansionary monetary policy because it results from nominal money growth, COIBION et al. (2012), on the other hand, have a result contrary to the long-term findings in ROMER and ROMER (1998), DAVTYAN (2016) and KANE and MORISETT (1993): Using the same data source for inequality measures that is employed in the following, the authors find that contractionary rather than expansionary monetary policy increase inequality. However, note that these authors employ a quarterly analysis rather than annual data and use a policy measure that controls for (expected) inflation (ROMER and ROMER, 2004) and thus tends to be orthogonal to changes in prices. These points may contribute to the divergent results.

In contrast to COIBION et al. (2012) and thus in coherence with KANE and MORISETT (1993), ROMER and ROMER (1998) and DAVTYAN (2016), SAIKI and FROST (2014) finds that expansionary monetary policy tends to increase inequality, even in the short-run, because the analyzed data only ranges from 2002 to 2014. Although there are parallels like the use of quarterly survey data and Vector Autoregressive Regression (VAR) analysis, the country under study in SAIKI and FROST (2014) is Japan rather than US. In addition, the focus lies on unconventional monetary policy instead of conventional monetary policy like it is measured by inflation or interest rates. SAIKI and

[1] OECD (2016), Producer price indices (PPI) (indicator). doi: 10.1787/a24f6fa9-en, accessed on 01.01.2017

FROST (2014) neither employs the so-called “Romer residuals” (ROMER and ROMER, 2004) like it is the case in COIBION et al. (2012), which are a measure of unexpected monetary policy but still rely on the Federal Funds Rate. Rather, the authors use the asset holdings of the Bank of Japan. The focus on unconventional monetary policy, which is reflected by an relief of liquidity conditions and private asset purchases that enlarge the central bank balance, is due to the binding zero lower bound of interest rates in Japan in that period. However, note that the stated tendency toward a positive effect of quantitative easing to inequality is the authors' reading of a positive point estimate, whereas the standard errors of their estimations are too high to ascertain significance.

ALBANESI (2002) reverses the causality between inequality and inflation in her political economy model. Nevertheless, she finds a positive correlation in a cross-sectional univariate regression analysis, using country averages over several years. GALBRAITH et al. (2007), in contrast, uses again annual US data from 1984 to 2003, and finds in a VAR regression that both, the FED's term structure expressed by the yield curve and the Consumer Price Index (CPI) inflation affect earnings inequality across 31 manufactoring sectors measured by the Theil index. Specifically, contractionary monetary policy as expressed by a flattening of the yield curve is found to increase inequality between the manufacturing sectors, thus the findings go into the same direction like those of COIBION et al. (2012). Similar to the analysis of the manufacturing sectors, IBRAHIM (2005) finds that interest rate changes have differently severe effects on different sectors of the Malaysian economy. Under labor market imperfections and/or segmentations that prevent workers to an economic sector where they are paid better, and/or different financial structures in the sectors, this implies an effect on income inequality, too. However, the direction of the effect depends on the characteristics and the composition of the economic sectors.

6.2 Own Course of Action

6.2.1 Methodology and Data

In order to assure that the empirical results do not depend on the measure of inequality, several measures are employed in order to check for robustness. The indicators of interest are the Gini coefficient, the Relative Median Poverty Gap (RMPG), the Quintile Share Ratio (QSR) and - because it is the measure in the theoretical model of the previous section - the (log-)variance. Complete population data, i.e. known “true” values for these measures, are not available, therefore the inequality measures are survey-weighted estimations from the Consumer Expenditure Survey (CES) Public Use Microdata (PUM) and are calculated using the `R`-package `laeken` (ALFONS and TEMPL,

2013).

The Gini coefficient is an inequality measure that takes into account the complete (empirical) income distribution, i.e. it is not based on specific quantiles like the RMPG and the QSR that only consider the lower tail of the distribution (and its relation to the upper tail respectively). The estimator of the Gini is

$$\widehat{\text{Gini}} = 100 \cdot \left(\frac{\sum_{i=1}^{n} 2\left(w_i y_i \sum_{j=1}^{n} w_j\right) - \sum_{i=1}^{n} w_i^2 y_i}{\left(\sum_{i=1}^{n} w_i\right) \sum_{i=1}^{n} w_i y_i} - 1 \right), \tag{0.1}$$

where w_i is the idiosyncratic survey-weight and y_i the variable of interest, i.e. here, it is either household pre-tax income or total expenditure, whose population mean is denoted by μ. The measure exploits the difference between an uniform distribution of income and the real total income shares of the population (ALFONS and TEMPL, 2013). This representation of the estimator differs slightly more from its population formula (for a discrete probability distribution f like it is the case for a discrete population of size N),

$$\text{Gini} = \frac{\sum_{i=1}^{N} \sum_{j=1}^{N} \left| y_i - y_j \right| f(y_i) f(y_j)}{2\mu}, \tag{6.2}$$

(GASTWIRTH, 1972) than the other estimators. In words, the Gini coefficient is defined as the ratio of the area between the Lorenz curve (that is exemplarily plotted in figure (6.9)) and the distribution function of the uniform distribution. The greater the ratio, the less the (income) distribution deviates from the uniform distribution, meaning income is less equally distributed.

The QSR on the other hand disregards the middle of the income distribution and contrasts the total income of the highest quintile with the total income of the lowest quintile:

$$\begin{aligned} \widehat{\text{QSR}} &= \frac{\sum_{i=1}^{n} 1_{y_i \geq \hat{\tau}_{0.8}} w_i y_i}{\sum_{i=1}^{n} 1_{y_i \leq \hat{\tau}_{0.2}} w_i y_i}, \\ \hat{F}(\hat{\tau}_q) &= q, \end{aligned} \tag{6.3}$$

where $\hat{F}$ is the empirical Cumulative Density Function (CDF) and $\hat{\tau}_q$ is the empirical q-quantile. Graphically, the QSR is the ratio between the right and the left colored space in figure (6.1), where $f(\cdot)$ is the density function of the variable of interest y. The RMPG finally is a measure that only considers the lower part of the income distribution,

$$\widehat{\text{RMPG}} = 100 \cdot \frac{0.6 \cdot \hat{\tau}_{0.5} - \hat{\tau}^{\star}}{0.6 \cdot \hat{\tau}_{0.5}} \tag{6.4}$$

$$\hat{F}|_{\{1 \leq i \leq n: y_i < 0.6 \hat{\tau}_{0.5}\}}(\hat{\tau}^{\star}) = 0.5, \tag{6.5}$$

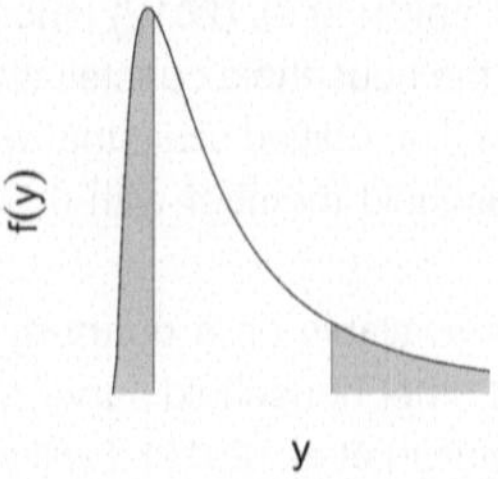

Figure 6.1: Illustration of the QSR

i.e. the relative difference of the median income of all observations considered to be poor, $\hat{\tau}^*$, to the poverty threshold, $0.6\hat{\tau}_{0.5}$. Finally, because it is the measure of inequality in the theoretical model, I consider the (estimated) variance of the equivalized income and expenditures. Due to the complex survey design, the estimator of choice is the weighted moment estimator,

$$\widehat{\text{Var}}(y_i) = \frac{\sum_{i=1}^{n} w_i y_i^2}{\sum_{i=1}^{n} w_i} - \left(\frac{\sum_{i=1}^{n} w_i y_i}{\sum_{i=1}^{n} w_i} \right)^2, \tag{6.6}$$

to incorporate easily the design-weights. Because the estimator (6.6) can theoretically become negative, but variances are always non-negative, setting the zero lower bound would be an option. However, this does not occur with the given data set. Note that the time subscript is omitted in formulas (6.1) to (6.6). These estimators are calculated for every quarter of the available CES files.

There is a high share of observations in the PUM that report zero total expenditure, and to a smaller extend, total income. While this does not present a problem for the Gini and the variance, it may happen that the lower quantiles are zero and this is problematic for indicators employing a ratio such as RMPG and QSR. Therefore, those observations are deleted; for comparison reasons even in the calculus of the Gini and the variance. The CES does not include the upper 1% of the income distribution that holds a relatively large part, thus the estimates used in the analysis will tend to underestimate total inequality in the US.

In order to account for different household sizes, equivalized variables are used, meaning that the houshold-level variable is weighted with the household size. The reasoning behind equivalization is that households with a higher income still can be depreviated if a overproportional number of household members live in the household. In the theoretical model, each household is of the same size, therefore this procedure might be important, too, to validate the model. However, note that there are also arguments against equivalization: Coibion et al. (2012) ignore equivalization in their main analysis because they interpret the household constellation as the result of a utility optimization problem. I use the OECD-modified scale that weights the head of household with 1, any additional adult household member with 0.5 and children under 16 years with 0.3 [2].

The CES is a survey that is available on a quarterly basis, which is a distinctive feature in comparison with most other household surveys. It follows a monthly rotating panel system. However, like Coibion et al. (2012), I will aggregate to quarters in order to stabilize the estimation and to enlarge the respective sample size. The PUM contains information on total quarterly household expenditure which I prefer to inequality measures based only on consumption of non-durables because the theoretical model in the previous section includes any household spending in the consumption good. In addition, and due to reasons given in the following, I consider total household pre-tax income.

Davtyan (2016) criticizes the use of the CES for measuring inequality since it does not contain the top 1% of the income distribution. However, the CES is available as public use microdata file from 1996 to 2014 and indicates in which quarter of the year a household has been interviewed. This allows to calculate quarterly inequality measures in contrast to the Current Population Survey she relies her analysis on. In addition, the quarterly data sums up to a total of 73 observation points after taking the necessary first differences. The annual analysis, on the other hand, as undergone in Davtyan (2016), may use other data sources that enclose the top tail of the income distribution. Nevertheless, inequality measures do not date back for very long such that the author must restrict herself to the time period from 1960 to 2012. This results in a total number of observations that is clearly below that of a quarterly analysis. As monetary policy is conducted more frequently, too, the annual data troubles an appropriate measure of monetary policy. Finally, some inequality measures like the RMPG do not even require information about the upper tail of the income distribution. Those arguments in favor of the CES outweigh the disadvantages in my point of view. Thus, I rely the empirical analysis on inequality measures from the CES.

Only the household expenditure has a quarterly reference period, though. Income variables, in contrast, refer to the previous 12 months. Nevertheless, this leads only to a partial overlap between two successive quarters so that a potential change in the distribution can be tracked. While the household expenditure is related to household income, there are two arguments about expenditure inequality that must be considered: First, households can (temporarily) maintain a certain expenditure/consumption level even after a negative income shock due to borrowing. This concern can be met by the

2 https://www.oecd.org/eco/growth/OECD-Note-EquivalenceScales.pdf, accessed on 07.01.2017

inclusion of the household Financial Obligation Ratio (FOR) in order to control for a possible rise in credit intake.

Second, households may have different marginal propensities to consume based on their income. A change in monetary policy therefore might create different consumption incentives to households and therefore expenditure inequality could understate inequality: For clarification, assume that expansionary monetary policy increases inequality, i.e. the richer households' income grows faster than the poorer households'. However, a lower propensity to consume for the richer households leads to a low consumption growth in the upper percentiles whereas the lower percentiles expand relatively much their consumption. Therefore, consumption inequality may grow slower or even reduce whereas income inequality has risen. Once again, the FOR may help: It puts the houshold's financial obligations into relation with its disposable income. When the income changes, the FOR changes, too, even when the credit level remains constant. This variable is thought to reduce the distortion from expenditure-based indicators that may come from different propensities to consume and/or consumption flattening. Additionally, when expansionary monetary policy is found to reduce expenditure inequality, then the understatement character of these measures may even robustify this finding. Additionally, the use of the RMPG does only rely on the lower part of the distribution such that this second effect should not be too large when this inequality measure is applied. Another way to ensure the robustness of my findings is the use of measures based on household income. Income is reported for the preceding 12 months, so there is still some information included about quarterly income changes because data only overlap partially.

Table (6.1) shows the correlation between the inequality measures using either the equivalized household income or equalized household expenditures and the FOR of households. It can be seen that the correlation between those measures relying on

Table 6.1: Correlation Table of Inequality Measures

	Gini-Inc	QSR-Inc	RMPG-Inc	Variance-Inc	Gini-Exp	QSR-Exp	RMPG-Exp	Variance-Exp	FOR
Gini-Inc	1.00	0.94	0.77	-0.45	0.53	0.85	0.40	-0.42	-0.21
QSR-Inc	0.94	1.00	0.92	-0.68	0.64	0.91	0.50	-0.52	-0.01
RMPG-Inc	0.77	0.92	1.00	-0.83	0.68	0.84	0.55	-0.57	0.18
Variance-Inc	-0.45	-0.68	-0.83	1.00	-0.68	-0.69	-0.53	0.63	-0.39
Gini-Exp	0.53	0.64	0.68	-0.68	1.00	0.70	0.53	-0.10	0.18
QSR-Exp	0.85	0.91	0.84	-0.69	0.70	1.00	0.55	-0.48	-0.01
RMPG-Exp	0.40	0.50	0.55	-0.53	0.53	0.55	1.00	-0.32	0.21
Variance-Exp	-0.42	-0.52	-0.57	0.63	-0.10	-0.48	-0.32	1.00	-0.11
FOR	-0.21	-0.01	0.18	-0.39	0.18	-0.01	0.21	-0.11	1.00

either income or expenditures is relatively high but sometimes negative. This might indicate that the concerns about the expenditure measure given above are justified. However, the correlation between the FOR and the income measures is moderate for the Gini coefficient, the RMPG and the variance and negative except for the RMPG.

This gives some confidence that the FOR might correct for additional borrowing after income shocks. Additionally, the varying signs of the correlation coefficients give an idea why analyzing the impact of monetary policy on inequality is difficult: The analysis always depends on the measure of inequality and consequently on the parts of the income/expenditure distribution that is focused. Hence, a robust statement about the effect should rely on qualitatively similar results irrespectively the measure of inequality and monetary policy that are employed.

There are different measures of monetary policy, too. DAVTYAN (2016) and ROMER and ROMER (1998) use the GDP (GNP) deflator based inflation rate. Inflation is the measure of monetary policy that is used in the theoretical model of the previous section. Nonetheless, actual monetary policy only influences the inflation rate indirectly via the short term interest rate. Therefore, I include the inflation rate based on the GDP deflator and the CPI in my analysis, but another monetary policy variable should be considered, too. COIBION et al. (2012) uses the monetary policy measure of ROMER and ROMER (2004). This measure takes as monetary policy the part of the Federal Funds Rate change that is not explained by deliberate (anticyclical) and anticipatory policy decisions, meaning that a regression on the Federal Funds Rate is run and the residuals are interpreted as "monetary shocks". Those may result from policy errors. However, these errors are predicted by residuals from a regression. Regressions bear the risk of miss-specification both in lag structure and omitted variables so that the residuals might be bad predictions/measures of monetary policy. Furthermore, those residuals are orthogonal to those macroeconomic variables included in the regression and therefore, their effect on those variables ought to be insignificant.

GALBRAITH et al. (2007) uses the FED's term structure expressed as the difference between the 30-day bill rate and the 10-year Treasury bond rate. Monetary policy takes effect on the short-term rate only, while the long-term rate includes inflation expectations. Thus, a change in the difference between the two, say a reduction means an increase in either the short-term rate or a decrease in the long-term rate. The former is a direct effect of a reduction in money supply whereas the latter expresses lower inflation expectations. Both go along with a contractionary monetary policy. Usually, the yield is positive, i.e. the long-term interest is higher than the short-term interest. This is due to inflation expectations, more insecurity the longer the time horizon is and a general individual discounting of future income flows. Therefore, an inversion may indicate an upcoming downward trend of the economy: When the monetary authority increases the short-term interest, i.e. conducts contractionary monetary policy, which is considered to slow down the economy (BOFINGER et al., 2001, pp. 282). Figure (6.2) plots the yield curve in the considered time period. Like in the theoretical explanation, the yield curve becomes negative in the preliminary of the 2000's recession and of the Great Recession. Hence, the term structure is a monetary policy measure that

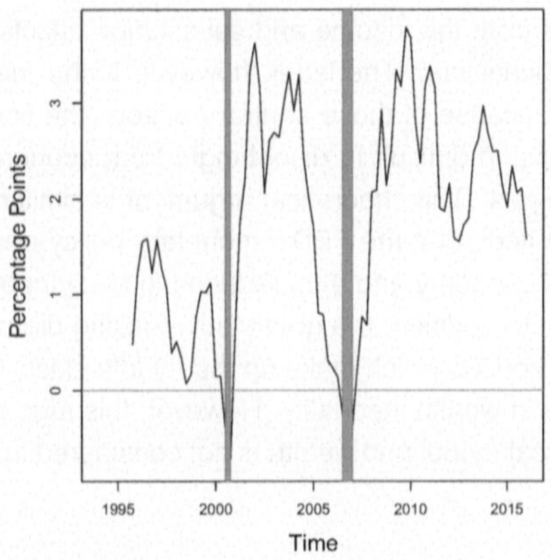

Figure 6.2: Time Series of the Yield Curve

goes beyond the inflation rate. In addition, it does not require the construction of an arguable regression model from which on uses the residuals. Therefore, I use the term structure as my measure choice in the analysis. However, due to data availability, the difference between the 10-year Treasure bond rate and the 3-month bill rate instead of the 1-month rate is employed.

As control variables, the quarterly unemployment rate, real GDP growth (seasonally adjusted) and a dummy for the Great Recession from the 4th quarter 2007 to the 2nd quarter 2009 are included. In consistency with the role of educational investment in the theoretical model, I also take into account the share of the population above 25 that have completed at least 4 years of highschool. Another variable that measures the population share who have completed at least 4 years of college returned worse results for the multivariate normality test, though the other results are similar. Therefore, the highschool variable is used. Finally, the FOR is included, too, for the reasons given above.

Like it has already been stated implicitly, I conduct a longitudinal analysis of US data. Specifically, VARs are used to uncover a possible relationship between monetary policy and inequality. Besides significance tests in order to assess the role of monetary policy, Impulse-Response Functions (IRFs) are used in longitudinal analysis to evaluate the effect of a one standard deviation shock in a variable. However, classical orthogonalized IRFs depend on the variable ordering in the underlying VAR. Therefore, I use generalized IRF like they were suggested in PESARAN and SHIN (1998).

As a last remark, note that the impact of monetary policy found in the previous section's model results from the income and substitution effects that translate to a divergent consumption behaviour. The latter, however, is the main driver of economic growth in the model. Because of those contrary effects, the final impact of monetary policy is rather indirect and difficult to disentangle from economic growth in the subsequent empirical analysis. This theoretical argument is similar to the argumentation in BIVENS (2015) who finds that the FED's monetary policy during the Great Recession stabilized the real economy and thus reduced income inequality compared to no monetary intervention. In addition, the quantitative easing did not only stabilize stock prices but also housing prices which make up the middle-class' wealth, therefore it did not trigger an increase in wealth inequality. However, this argument is not wrapped in the introduced theoretical model and wealth is not considered in the empirical analysis neither.

6.2.2 Results

Univariate time series plots as part of the summary statistics can be found in appendix D. Like it has been suggested in the previous paragraph, the results of the VAR analysis are ambiguous. Using the Akaike Information Criterion (AIC), which tends to overstate the optimal lag order, the latter never exceeds 2 lags which is a good result because the variety of included variables and the relative small period of observation requires scarcity. In addition, this lag order is smaller than suggested by the maximum order univariate Ljung and Box tests. Because the univariate analysis has returned ambiguous results concerning the stationarity of the first difference of the population share who have completed at least 4 years of highschool, second differences of that variable are employed in the analysis. The Augmented Dickey Fuller test (ADF), involving a dummy for the Great Recession, however, finds that in the univariate case a deterministic trend is necessary to maintain mean stationarity. Hence, the deterministic trend was included in the VARs, too.

None of the preferred VAR models reveals autocorrelation or heteroskedasticity in the multivariate distribution of the residuals. In the case of the income-measured inequality indicators, the hypothesis of both, univariate and multivariate normality of the residuals cannot be rejected in the Jarque-Bera test.

The analysis of the indicators based on total household expenditure, in contrast, are more problematic in the multivariate analysis. In order to account for increased indebtedness of households that suffer from an income shock, the FOR was included. However, already the time series plot (6.3) suggests that the normality assumption (of the error term) would be difficult to accept, the more probable as the time series analysis is linear in the endogenous variables and none of the other univariate time series in appendix D reveals a similar movement. Univariate Jarque-Bera tests affirm that it is in

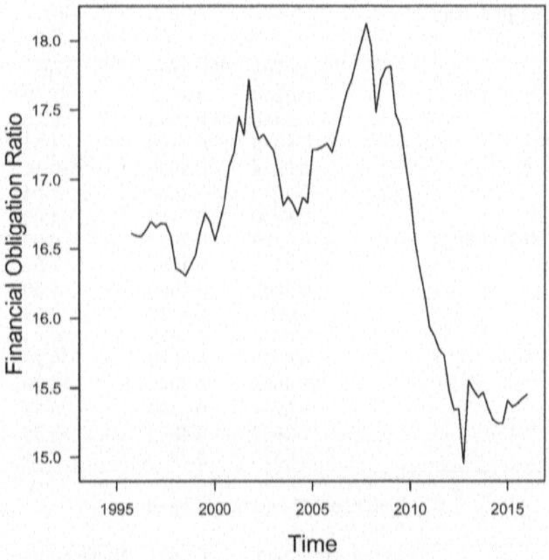

Figure 6.3: Financial Obligation Ratio of Households

fact the regression on FOR that makes the test statistic critical. In order to check for the need to include the FOR, I re-estimated the VAR that includes the Gini coefficient of total expenditures without FOR. This really allows to accept the hypothesis of normally distributed residuals. However, likelihood ratio tests that contrast every single regression with its counterpart that includes the FOR suggest that a non-negligible amount of information gets lost when the FOR is omitted. Thus, for the reasons given in the previous section about the consumption behaviour and because of the likelihood ratio tests, I keep the FOR in the analysis even though it hurts the normality assumption. Only the log-QSR based on expenditure has troubles about the normality assumption even in the univariate analysis. However, neither the untransformed QSR nor the inclusion of an additional dummy variable (cf. the time series in figure (D.9)) has solved the problem. Thus, in consistency with the income-based VARs, I keep the log-QSR. Table (6.2) summarizes the VAR regression on the income-based Gini coefficient. Obivously, the yield is neither significant in the first nor the second lag. However, they are commonly significant at the 10% threshold, as the F-test under the regression summary of table (6.2) reveals. The rest of the VAR regressions on the other inequality measures are reported in appendix E. Nevertheless, when testing the overall effect of the term structure, $\beta_{Yield.L1} + \beta_{Yield.L2}$, the null hypothesis of non-negativity must be accepted, although both coefficients have negative point estimates. Therefore, the regression above suggests that the yield has an effect on inequality measured by the Gini coefficient, but the direction of the effect is not clear-cut. This is also illustrated in figure (6.4) which plots the IRF of yield on the Gini coefficient. Only after 3 quarters the ef-

Table 6.2: Regression on Gini-Inc

	Estimate	Std. Error	t value	Pr(> $|t|$)	
Completed ≥ 4 Years in Highschool-2nd Diff. L1	-0.2804	0.2122	-1.32	0.1913	
GDP Growth L1	0.3450	0.1544	2.23	0.0290	**
Unemployment Rate L1	0.6445	0.4198	1.54	0.1299	
GDP Deflator L1	-0.0664	0.4030	-0.16	0.8697	
Yield L1	-0.1535	0.1481	-1.04	0.3040	
Gini-Inc L1	0.4700	0.1166	4.03	0.0002	***
Completed ≥ 4 Years in Highschool-2nd Diff. L2	0.1786	0.2013	0.89	0.3783	
GDP Growth L2	0.3179	0.1662	1.91	0.0605	*
Unemployment Rate L2	-0.6085	0.4060	-1.50	0.1390	
GDP Deflator L2	0.4094	0.4125	0.99	0.3249	
Yield L2	-0.0648	0.1479	-0.44	0.6626	
Gini-Inc L2	-0.0749	0.1043	-0.72	0.4751	
const	26.9606	4.7348	5.69	0.0000	***
trend	0.0254	0.0095	2.68	0.0093	***
Variable Rupture	-2.3839	0.4295	-5.55	0.0000	***
Great Recession	0.6310	0.3920	1.61	0.1125	
Signif. codes:	'***' 0.01 '**' 0.05 '*' 0.1				
Residual standard error:	0.6035 on 62 degrees of freedom				
Multiple R-squared:	0.8429,			Adjusted R-squared:	0.8049
JB-test, p-value:	Single regression:	0.5447	Multivariate:		0.938
Portemanteau-test	pvalue:	0.1675			
ARCH-test, p-value:	Single regression:	0.7577	Multivariate:		1
F-statistic:	22.17 on 15 and 62 DF,			p-value:	$< 2.2e-16$
F-statistic $H_0 : \begin{cases} \beta_{Yield.L1} = 0 \\ \beta_{Yield.L2} = 0 \end{cases}$	3.0089 on 2 and 62 DF,			p-value:	0.0566
t-statistic $H_0 : \beta_{Yield.L1} + \beta_{Yield.L2} \geq 0$	-0.7740 on 62 DF,			p-value:	0.7791

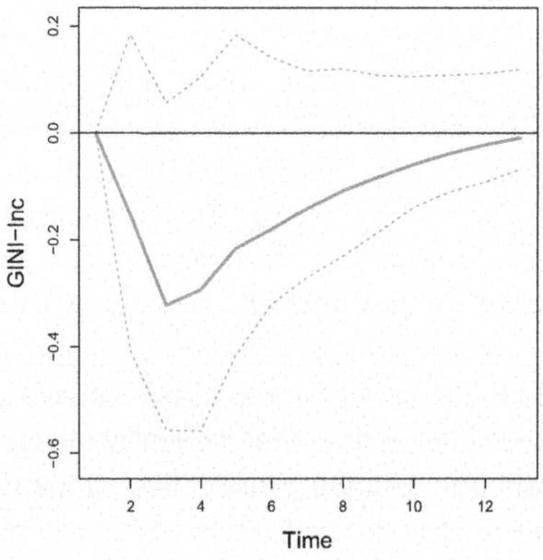

Figure 6.4: IRF of Yield on Gini-Inc

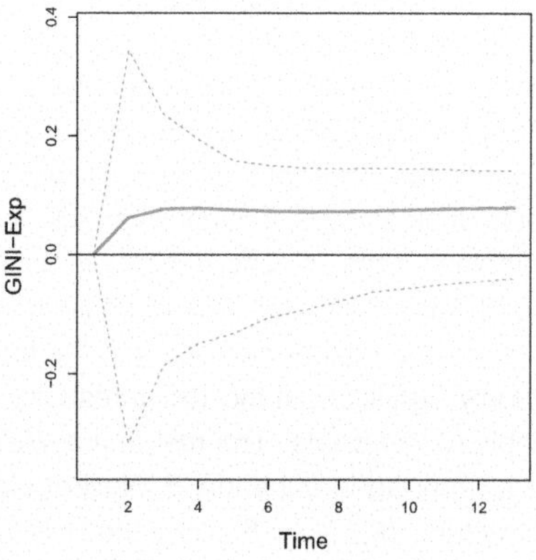

Figure 6.5: IRF of Yield on Gini-Exp

fect of a change in the term structure gets close to significance (and is so at the 10% threshold). However, in tendency, one might say that an increase in the yield, meaning expansionary monetary policy, reduces the Gini coefficient, i.e. reduces inequality. A similar behaviour is observed for the RMPG and the (logarithmic) QSR based on the income variable, cf. tables (E.1), (E.2) and figures (F.1) and (F.2). However, there, the rather non-positive impact of the yield, i.e. of expansionary monetary policy, is a little more evident. Nevertheless, these findings are not backed by the regression on the (logarithmic) income variance as reported in the appendix (table (E.3) and figure (6.6)). Though those results are not strong enough to state a negative effect of contractionary monetary policy on equality, the tendency of these first results goes into the same direction like COIBION et al. (2012), which might be due to the use of the same data set and the application of VARs although the final inequality and monetary policy measures differ from COIBION et al. (2012).

Overall, one cannot tell distinctively about the direction of monetary policy, but the weak significances in the regressions (6.2), (E.1) and (E.2) rather suggests that expansionary monetary policy reduces income-based inequality at least in the short-run. Note, however, that the IRFs of the logarithmic income variance - figures (6.6) and (6.7) - shows a peak in the opposite direction, though the movement is not significant. This is in coherence with the suggestion of the previous section that expansionary monetary policy temporarily increases in tendency the second moment. As expansionary monetary policy was understood as inflation in the previous section, both IRFs are plotted here. One reason why the inequality measures show different sensitivity to the

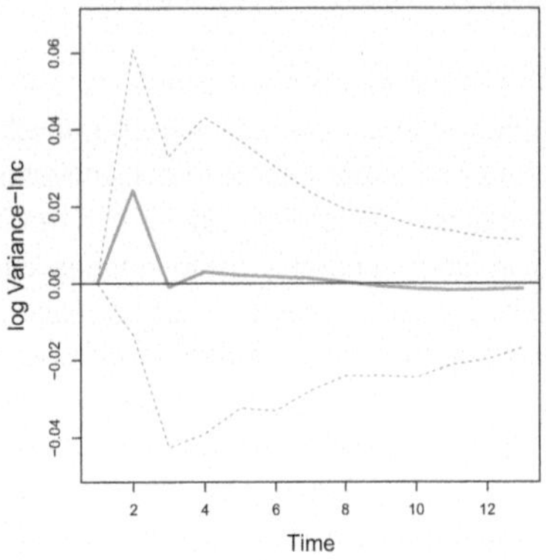

Figure 6.6: IRF of Yield on log Variance-Inc

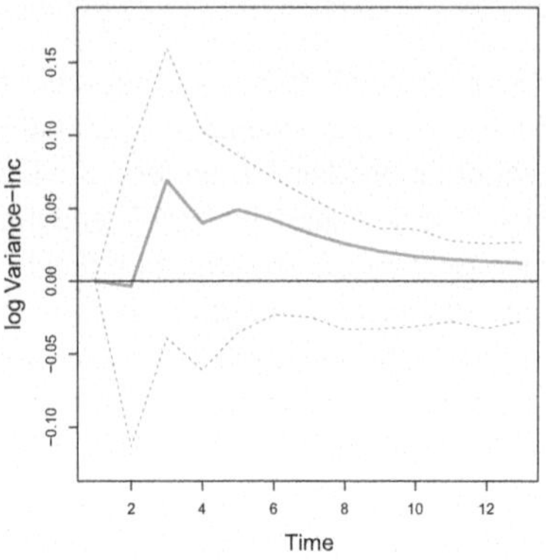

Figure 6.7: IRF of Inflation on log Variance-Inc

monetary policy measure might be the divergent weight they put on different income quantiles: The Gini coefficient considers the whole income distribution but in contrast to the variance measure that calculates the squared deviation from the mean, it considers the relative deviation among the individuals, i.e. not from the mean. Thus, a wider gap between the lowest and the highest quantile gets greater weight than in the variance measure. This effect is even more underlined with the RMPG and the QSR. The RMPG only considers the income distribution restricted to those under the poverty threshold, which is itself determined by the median. The QSR finally is the ratio between to quintiles, hence even more focusing on the tails of the distribution. Figure

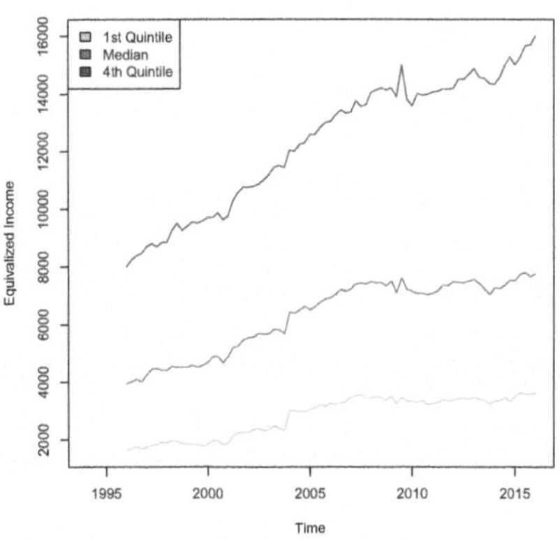

Figure 6.8: Time Series of Income Quantiles

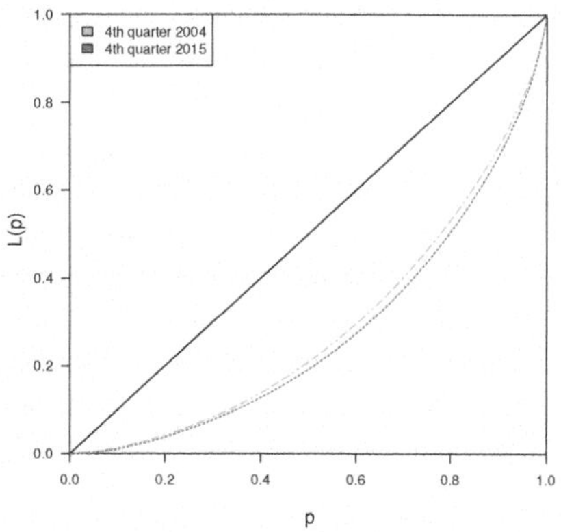

Figure 6.9: Lorenz Curve of Income

(6.8) illustrates that the gap between the first and the fourth quintile has remarkably widened over the time period considered, especially in comparison with the development of the median. Therefore, the QSR has shown a more accentuated movement across the time than the RMPG and therefore may reveal more sensitivity with respect to the yield curve. This might be due to diverging intertemporal substitution elasticities across the income quantiles, too. The change of the Lorenz curve, which is related to the Gini coefficient, plotted in figure (6.9), shows that there has gone more mass to the tails of the income distribution in a period of growing differences between the short- and long-run interests (cf. figure (6.2)). However, this slight change between 2004 and 2015 may not be statistically significant; remember that those measures rely on a survey rather than population values. This divergent focuses on the loci of the income distribution may explain the diverging results at least in parts.

Things look slightly different when considering expenditure inequality. Table (6.3)

reveals that the term structure has no longer a significant direct impact on the Gini coefficient. Neither has it an indirect impact via the other, significant variables in the VAR system, following the IRF (6.5).

However, note that an increase in the FOR reduces inequality of expenditure and is highly significant. This might indicate that households really compensate a temporary income shock with borrowing in order to maintain their consumption level and therefore, the expenditure inequality is not directly affected by the term structure. In the regression of the VAR-variables on FOR, the unemployment rate is the only additional variable that has an signifcant impact on FOR. For most individuals, becoming unemployed is still an important negative income shock and linked to a sharp decrease in disposable income, thus aggravating inequality, which underpins the hypothesis. In all

Table 6.3: Regression on Gini-Exp

	Estimate	Std. Error	t value	$Pr(>\|t\|)$	
Completed $\geq$ 4 Years in Highschool-2nd Diff. L1	0.0077	0.2137	0.04	0.9712	
GDP Growth L1	-0.1010	0.1880	-0.54	0.5929	
Unemployment Rate L1	-0.1886	0.1040	-1.81	0.0742	*
FOR L1	-0.5377	0.1553	-3.46	0.0009	***
GDP Deflator L1	-0.8561	0.5138	-1.67	0.1002	
Yield L1	0.0615	0.1148	0.54	0.5938	
GINI-Exp L1	0.0566	0.1176	0.48	0.6317	
const	52.9631	6.5745	8.06	0.0000	***
trend	-0.0127	0.0094	-1.36	0.1795	
Great Recession	-1.6433	0.5096	-3.22	0.0019	***
Signif. codes:	'***' 0.01 '**' 0.05 '*' 0.1				
Residual standard error:	0.8507 on 69 degrees of freedom				
Multiple R-squared:	0.6766,			Adjusted R-squared:	0.6344
JB-test, p-value:	Single regression:	0.5345	Multivariate:		0.01348
Portemanteau-test	pvalue:	0.2113			
ARCH-test, p-value:	Single regression:	0.7691	Multivariate:		1
F-statistic:	16.04 on 9 and 69 DF,			p-value:	$8.422e-14$

other regressions on expenditure-based inequality measures except for the logarithmic variance, the term structure is not significant neither. Furthermore, it is remarkable that not even the sign of the yield coefficient neither among the expenditure-based measures nor across the expenditure-income regressions show the same direction. Hence, the slight tendency towards a short-run inequality reduction through expansionary monetary policy that was suggested from the income-based measures is not backed by the expenditure based measures. However, note that the latter have in general less explanatory power than the former as inidcated by the adjusted R^2 and face some troubles about the model assumptions because of the inclusion of the FOR.

Finally, note that the VAR analysis takes into account the impact that monetary policy has on macroeconomic variables such as the unemployment rate and economic growth which affect inequality on their turn. This is what BIVENS (2015) requires for any discussion the link between monetary policy and inequality. Though not further discussed here, the IRFs from the yield curve on GDP growth and the unemployment rate have been plotted. They do not reveal significance, though.

Nevertheless, the IRFs take into account direct and indirect second round effects for more than one period ahead simulations. They show confidence bands that are too wide for conventional significance levels. Therefore, the stated effects of opposite sign, especially income and substitution effect, found in the introduced theoretical model seem to roughly balance each other, at least in the US from 1995 to 2015. Nevertheless, the VARs analyze the impact of a change in the term structure, hence it is a comparison to *no change*, the status quo. As BIVENS (2015) notes, another reasonable benchmark would be a fiscal policy instrument with a similar macroeconomic amplitude (in terms of GDP) like the interest rate change.

7 Conclusion

The research on the interdependencies of monetary policy and inequality is still a vivid field in economics. Especially the unconventional monetary policies conducted in industrial nations in the subsequent of economic stagnation and/or crisis has revitalized the discussion about the non-neutrality of money. Rather than to consider simply the income distribution's first moment, i.e. the mean, the shape of the whole distribution might be of interest to policy makers: AUCLERT (2014) raises the importance of inequality on the outcome of monetary policy measures. However, due to the circular flows in the economy, the effect of monetary policy on the income distribution is a point of interest per se.

While there are several (computational intensive) DSGE approaches using a NK framework to answer the question, some researchers have sought to disentangle the connection between monetary policy and income inequality analytically; amongst them JIN (2010). Based on his work, an endogenous growth model has been introduced that shows the effect that a raise in inflation has on the economy: When the inflation shock remains within a specific range, the economy returns to its BGP. This return is linked to a transitory change in the wage and interest rate growth from the instantaneously risen/fallen level to its original level. These transitory movements make agents act according to their policy rule. However, though all agents follow the same policy rule, the outcome diverges because they have different initial endowments of skill and capital. As the income effect is less pronounced for agents with less capital holdings, their behavior is mainly ruled by the substitution effect. Therefore, until the economy has returned to its BGP, the housholds' transitory reaction is divergent and finally equalizes on the BGP. Consequently, back on the BGP, there is no reversion of the transitory effects and the income variation has permanently changed. Because both, income and substitution effect, work on capital *and* labor income, a monetary policy shock can imply an increased correlation between human capital and asset holdings, even if the initial endowment was random and independent.

Unfortunately, the empirical analysis could not back the theoretical findings. The CES PUM is used to estimate several inequality measures based on equivalized household income and expenditure. Using VARs, that include the interest yield as variable of monetary policy and several controls, I could not get overall consistent results. Taking into account the effects of contrary sign elaborated in the theoretical model, though, this does not exclude significant results for other countries than the US and/or another time period of analysis, because the relative size of income and substitution effect depends on the original level of endowments that is regionally and/or longitudinally variable. Taking this into consideration, one possible explanation of the empirical result is that given the initial income/expenditure distribution in the US in 1995, both effects roughly

P. Dörr, *The Impact of Monetary Policy on Economic Inequality*,
BestMasters, https://doi.org/10.1007/978-3-658-24835-2_7

outweigh.
The relation between monetary policy and income inequality remains a wide field of economic research and there are several options to enlarge the introduced model: For example, households could choose between different options to invest their capital. The topic of (labor) market segmentation has been outlined only roughly. Finally, the introduced economy was closed: Implications may change when households can invest abroud or when exchange rates and hence exporting industries depond on inflation and nominal interest rate changes.

References

Albanesi, S. (**2002**): *Inflation and Inequality*. Technical report 3470, CEPR Discussion Papers.

Alfons, A. and **Templ, M.** (**2013**): *Estimation of Social Exclusion Indicators from Complex Surveys: The R Package laeken*. Journal of Statistical Software, 54 (15), pp. 1–25.
URL `http://www.jstatsoft.org/v54/i15/`

Auclert, A. (**2014**): *Monetary policy and the redistribution channel*. Unpublished Manuscript, Massachusetts Institute of Technology.

Bivens, J. (**2015**): *Gauging the impact of the Fed on inequality during the Great Recession*. Hutchins Center for Fiscal Monetary Policy Working Paper, 12.

Bofinger, P., **Reischle, J.** and **Schächter, A.** (**2001**): Monetary policy: goals, institutions, strategies, and instruments. Oxford University Press on Demand.

Castaneda, A., **Díaz-Giménez, J.** and **Ríos-Rull, J.-V.** (**2003**): *Accounting for the US earnings and wealth inequality*. Journal of Political Economy, 111 (4), pp. 818–857.

Coibion, O., **Gorodnichenko, Y.**, **Kueng, L.** and **Silvia, J.** (**2012**): *Innocent bystanders? Monetary policy and inequality in the US*. Technical report, National Bureau of Economic Research.

Da Costa, C. E. and **Werning, I.** (**2008**): *On the optimality of the Friedman rule with heterogeneous agents and nonlinear income taxation*. Journal of Political Economy, 116 (1), pp. 82–112.

Davtyan, K. (**2016**): *Income Inequality and Monetary Policy: An Analysis on the Long Run Relation*. Technical report, University of Barcelona, Regional Quantitative Analysis Group.

Deininger, K. and **Squire, L.** (**1998**): *New ways of looking at old issues: inequality and growth*. Journal of development economics, 57 (2), pp. 259–287.

Demekas, D. G. (**1990**): *Labor market segmentation in a two-sector model of an open economy*. Staff Papers, IMF, 37 (4), pp. 849–864.

Doepke, M., **Schneider, M.** and **Selezneva, V.** (**2015**): *Distributional effects of monetary policy*. Unpublished manuscript.

P. Dörr, *The Impact of Monetary Policy on Economic Inequality*,
BestMasters, https://doi.org/10.1007/978-3-658-24835-2

Easterly, W. and **Fischer, S.** (**2001**): *Inflation and the Poor.* Journal of Money, Credit and Banking, pp. 160–178.

Galbraith, J. K., **Giovannoni, O. G.** and **Russo, A. J.** (**2007**): *The Fed's Real Reaction Function Monetary Policy, Inflation, Unemployment, Inequality-and Presidential Politics.* Technical report.

Galí, J. (**2015**): Monetary policy, inflation, and the business cycle: an introduction to the new Keynesian framework and its applications. Princeton University Press.

Gali, J. and **Monacelli, T.** (**2005**): *Monetary policy and exchange rate volatility in a small open economy.* The Review of Economic Studies, 72 (3), pp. 707–734.

García-Peñalosa, C. and **Turnovsky, S. J.** (**2006**): *Growth and income inequality: a canonical model.* Economic Theory, 28 (1), pp. 25–49.

Gastwirth, J. L. (**1972**): *The estimation of the Lorenz curve and Gini index.* The review of economics and statistics, pp. 306–316.

Gertler, M. and **Karadi, P.** (**2009**): *A Model of Unconventional Monetary Policy.*

Gornemann, N., **Kuester, K.** and **Nakajima, M.** (**2012**): *Monetary policy with heterogeneous agents.*

Greenwood, J. and **Jovanovic, B.** (**1989**): *Financial development, growth, and the distribution of income.* Technical report, National Bureau of Economic Research.

Heer, B. and **Maussner, A.** (**2009**): Dynamic general equilibrium modeling: computational methods and applications. Springer Science & Business Media.

Huggett, M. (**1996**): *Wealth distribution in life-cycle economies.* Journal of Monetary Economics, 38 (3), pp. 469–494.

Ibrahim, M. H. (**2005**): *Sectoral effects of monetary policy: evidence from Malaysia.* Asian Economic Journal, 19 (1), pp. 83–102.

Jin, Y. (**2009**): *A note on inflation, economic growth, and income inequality.* Macroeconomic Dynamics, 13 (1), p. 138.

Jin, Y. (**2010**): *Growth, Inflation, and Inequality in a Monetary Two-Sector Endogenous Growth Model.* Technical report, Monash University, Department of Economics.

Kane, C. and **Morisett, J.** (**1993**): *Who would vote for inflation in Brazil?* Policy Research Working Paper, 1183.

Kaplan, G., **Moll, B.** and **Violante, G. L.** (**2016**): *Monetary policy according to HANK.* Technical report, National Bureau of Economic Research.

Lee, J. W. (**2010**): *Monetary Policy with Heterogeneous Households and Imperfect Risk-Sharing.* Available at SSRN 1546728.

Longaretti, R., **Gatti, D. D.** et al. (**2006**): *The Non-Superneutrality of Money and its Distributional Effects when Agents are Heterogeneous and Capital Markets are Imperfect.* Technical report.

Mathai, K. (**2009**): *What is monetary policy?* Finance & Development, 46, pp. 46–47.

Meh, C. A., **Ríos-Rull, J.-V.** and **Terajima, Y.** (**2008**): *Aggregate and Welfare Effects of Redistribution of Wealth Under Inflation and Price-Level Targeting.*

Palivos, T. (**2004**): *Optimal monetary policy with heterogeneous agents: a case for inflation.* Oxford Economic Papers.

Pesaran, H. H. and **Shin, Y.** (**1998**): *Generalized impulse response analysis in linear multivariate models.* Economics letters, 58 (1), pp. 17–29.

Rochon, L.-P. and **Setterfield, M.** (**2007**): *Interest rates, income distribution, and monetary policy dominance: Post Keynesians and the" fair rate" of interest.* Journal of Post Keynesian Economics, 30 (1), pp. 13–42.

Romer, C. D. and **Romer, D. H.** (**1998**): *Monetary policy and the well-being of the poor.* Technical report, National Bureau of Economic Research.

Romer, C. D. and **Romer, D. H.** (**2004**): *A new measure of monetary shocks: Derivation and implications.* The American Economic Review, 94 (4), pp. 1055–1084.

Saiki, A. and **Frost, J.** (**2014**): *Does unconventional monetary policy affect inequality? Evidence from Japan.* Applied Economics, 46 (36), pp. 4445–4454.

Wälde, K. (**2011**): Applied Intertemporal Optimization, Edition 1.1. Available at www.waelde.com/aio: Mainz University Gutenberg Press.

Williamson, S. D. (**2008**): *Monetary Policy and Distribution.*

Appendices

A Skill, Interest and Wage Change

Table A.1: Correlation Table - Skill, Interest and Wage Change

	Growth of tertiary education	Growth of av. income	Long Term Interest Rate
Growth of tertiary education	1.00	−0.04	0.02
Growth of av. income	−0.04	1.00	−0.27
Long Term Interest Rate	0.02	−0.27	1.00

Source: Data downloaded from http://stat.oecd.org on 13.11.2016

B Proof that $\frac{\dot{E}}{E} = 0$

The aggregate labor growth can be described as

$$\frac{\dot{L}}{L} = \frac{\dot{S}}{S}\frac{S}{S-E} - \frac{\dot{E}}{E}\frac{E}{S-E} = \frac{i-\rho}{\sigma} \qquad \Leftrightarrow$$
$$\frac{\dot{E}}{E} = \delta - \frac{i-\rho}{\sigma}\frac{S-E}{E}. \tag{B.1}$$

Analogously to (5.46), the aggregate no Ponzi game condition for human capital accumulation is

$$\lim_{t\to\infty} \exp(-\rho t)\bar{\mu}(t)S(t) = 0 \qquad \Leftrightarrow \qquad \frac{\dot{\mu}}{\mu} + \frac{\dot{S}}{S} - \rho \leq 0, \tag{B.2}$$

leading to

$$\frac{\dot{S}}{S} = \delta\frac{E}{S} < \delta. \tag{B.3}$$

Exploiting the BC (5.5) and the CIA (5.6), we can rewrite the time investment in education as

$$e_h = s_h + \frac{i}{w_j}a_h - \frac{1}{w_j}\dot{a}_h - \frac{1}{w_j}\dot{m}_h. \tag{B.4}$$

On the BGP, we get thus on the individual and the aggregate level respectively:

$$\dot{e}_h = \dot{s}_h + \frac{i}{w_j}\dot{a}_h = \delta e_h + \frac{i}{w_j}\dot{a}_h \tag{B.5}$$
$$\dot{E} = \delta E + i\left(\frac{1}{w_1}\frac{L_1}{L} + \frac{1}{w_2}\frac{L_2}{L}\right)\dot{K}. \tag{B.6}$$

With $h(x) = x^{-1}$ being a convex function and average wage $\overline{w}$, it follows that $1 \leq \overline{w}\left(\frac{1}{w_1}\frac{L_1}{L} + \frac{1}{w_2}\frac{L_2}{L}\right) =: \xi$ and thus, we can derive with equation (B.1) that

$$E = S + \frac{i}{\overline{w}}\frac{\sigma}{i-\rho}\xi\dot{K} = S + \frac{i}{\overline{w}}\xi K > S. \tag{B.7}$$

However, this is a contradiction to the no Ponzi-game condition (B.3). □

P. Dörr, *The Impact of Monetary Policy on Economic Inequality*,
BestMasters, https://doi.org/10.1007/978-3-658-24835-2

C Average Education Spending

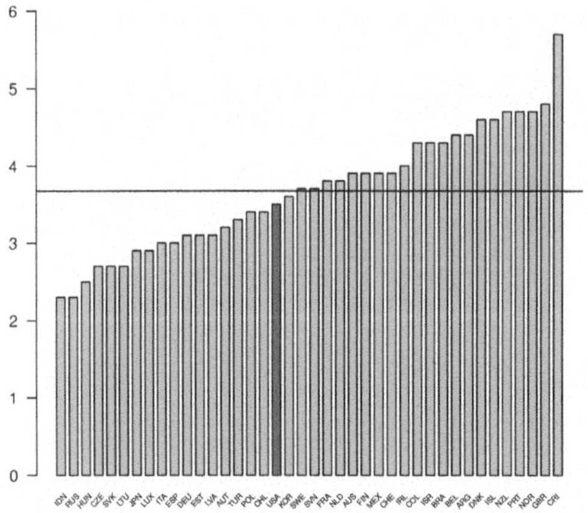

Figure C.1: Education Spending in OECD Countries, Percent of GDP

Source: Data downloaded from https://data.oecd.org/eduresource/education-spending.htm on 10.12.2016

D Time Series Plots

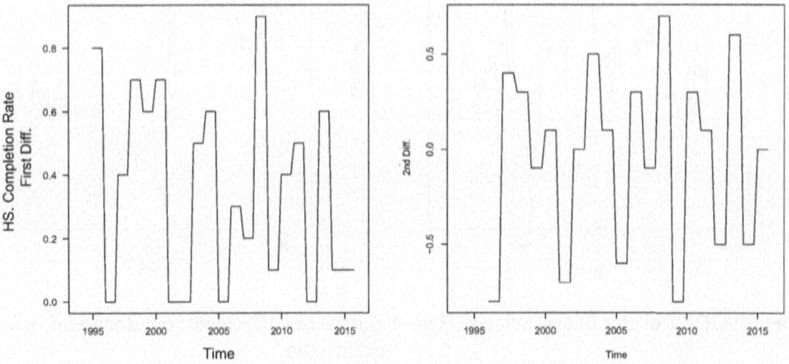

Figure D.1: Share of Population that Completed at least 4 Years of Highschool - First and Second Differences

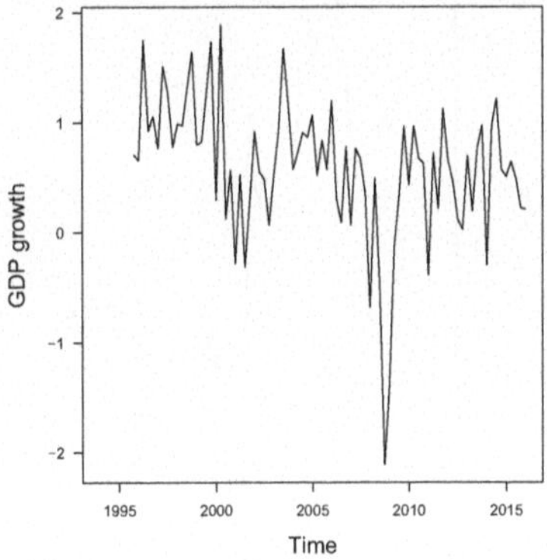

Figure D.2: GDP Growth

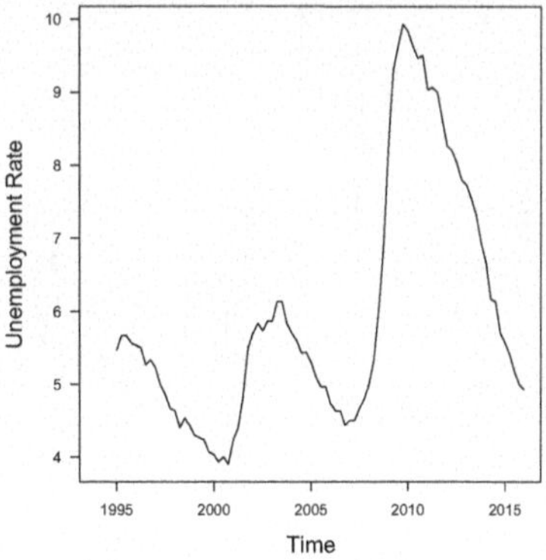

Figure D.3: Unemployment Rate

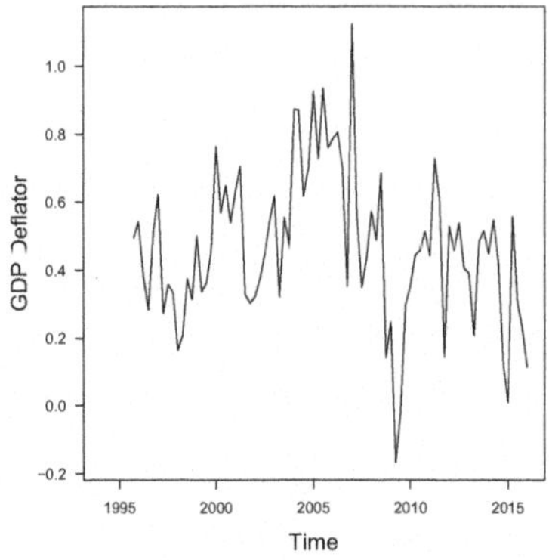

Figure D.4: GDP Deflator Based Inflation Rate

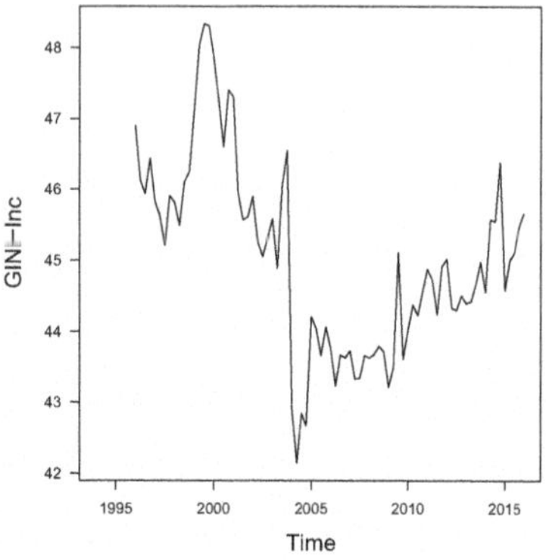

Figure D.5: GINI Coefficient Based on Household Income

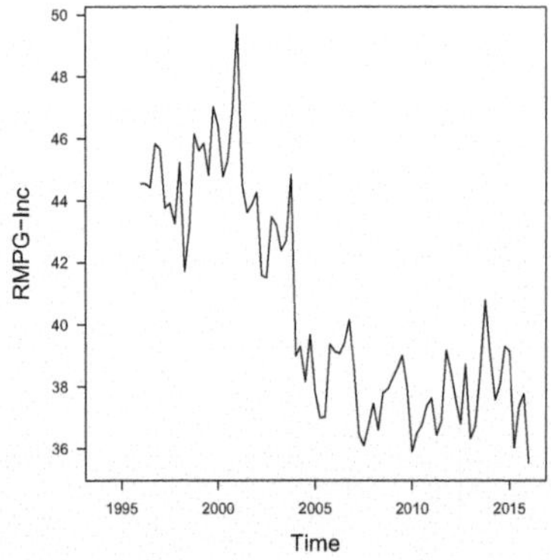

Figure D.6: RMPG Based on Household Income

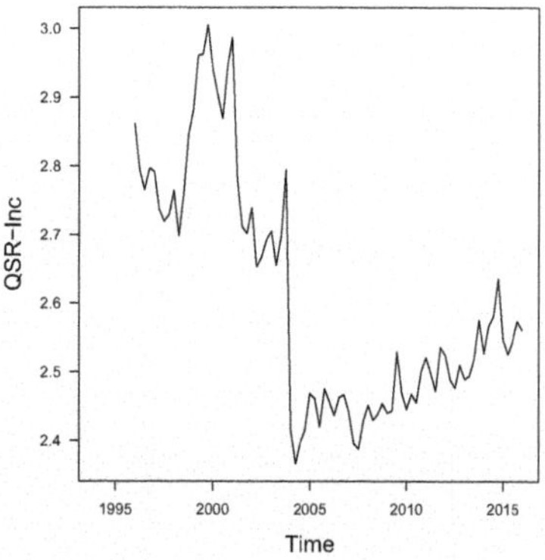

Figure D.7: log QSR Based on Household Income

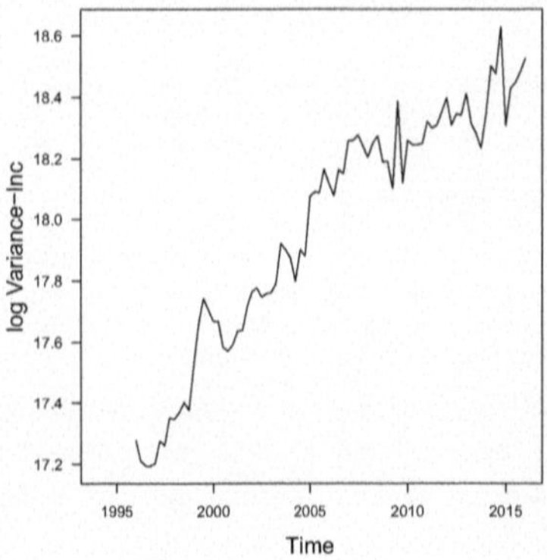

Figure D.8: log Variance of Household Income

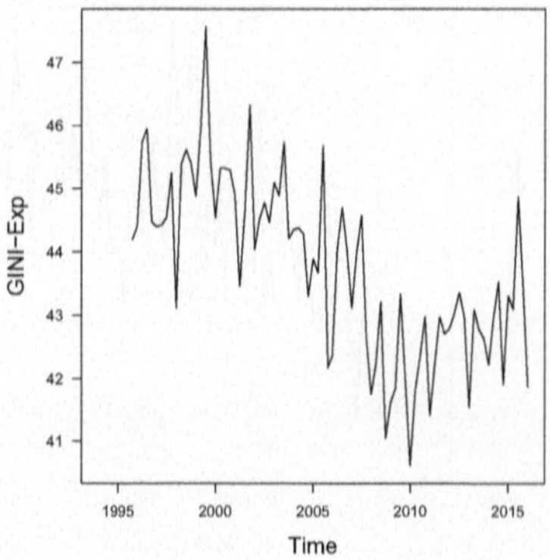

Figure D.9: GINI Coefficient Based on Total Household Expenditure

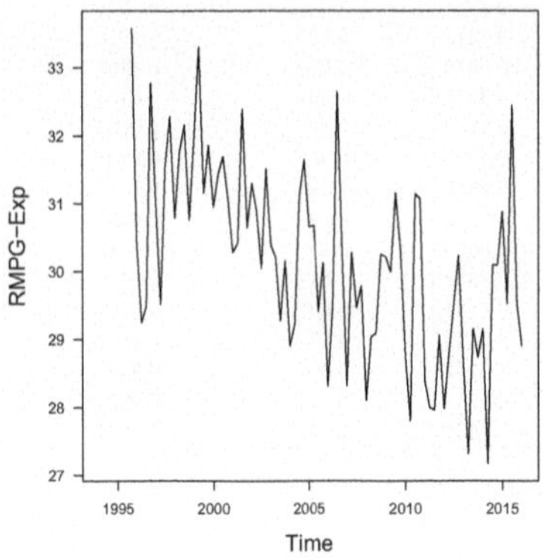

Figure D.10: RMPG Based on Total Household Expenditure

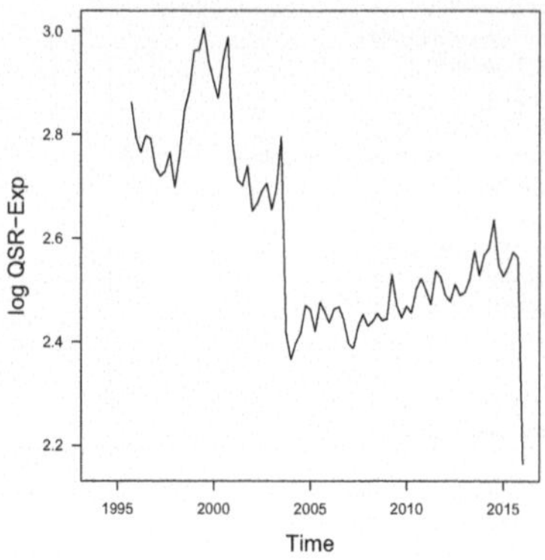

Figure D.11: log QSR Based on Total Household Expenditure

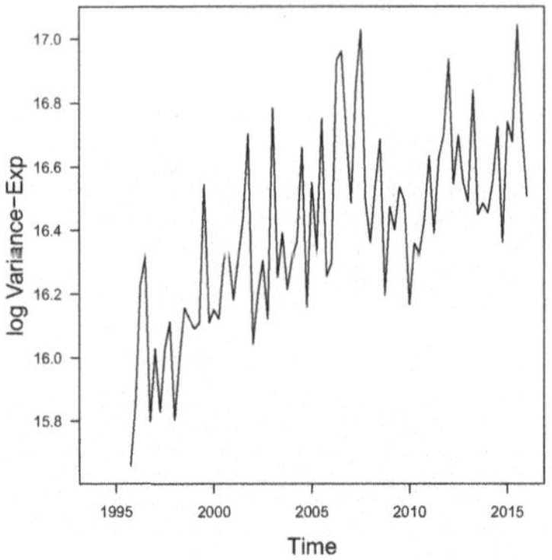

Figure D.12: log Variance of Total Household Expenditure

E Regression Results

Table E.1: Regression on RMPG-Inc

	Estimate	Std. Error	t value	Pr(> $\|t\|$)	
Completed ≥ 4 Years in Highschool-2nd Diff. L1	-0.2833	0.4594	-0.62	0.5397	
GDP Growth L1	0.4771	0.3352	1.42	0.1596	
Unemployment Rate L1	0.6300	0.9213	0.68	0.4966	
GDP Deflator L1	0.7301	0.8919	0.82	0.4161	
Yield L1	-0.8776	0.3314	-2.65	0.0103	**
RMPG-Inc L1	0.4425	0.1157	3.82	0.0003	***
Completed ≥ 4 Years in Highschool-2nd Diff. L2	0.4225	0.4397	0.96	0.3403	
GDP Growth L2	-0.1146	0.3606	-0.32	0.7517	
Unemployment Rate L2	-0.6990	0.8870	-0.79	0.4337	
GDP Deflator L2	0.4756	0.9068	0.52	0.6018	
Yield L2	0.6022	0.3327	1.81	0.0751	*
RMPG-Inc L2	-0.0716	0.1141	-0.63	0.5323	
const	27.9478	5.7338	4.87	0.0000	***
trend	-0.0013	0.0203	-0.06	0.9486	
Variable Rupture	-4.4462	0.8652	-5.14	0.0000	***
Great Recession	0.9581	0.8381	1.14	0.2574	
Signif. codes:	'***' 0.01 '**' 0.05 '*' 0.1				
Residual standard error:	1.304 on 62 degrees of freedom				
Multiple R-squared:	0.8899,			Adjusted R-squared:	0.8633
JB-test, p-value:	Single regression:	0.8171	Multivariate:		0.9719
Portemanteau-test, pvalue:	0.2302				
ARCH-test, p-value:	Single regression:	0.5091	Multivariate:		1
F-statistic:	33.42 on 15 and 62 DF,			p-value:	$< 2.2e-16$
F-statistic $H_0 : \begin{cases} \beta_{Yield.L1} = 0 \\ \beta_{Yield.L2} = 0 \end{cases}$	3.7251 on 2 and 62 DF,			p-value:	0.02967
t-statistic $H_0 : \beta_{Yield.L1} + \beta_{Yield.L2} \geq 0$	-0.4341 on 62 DF,			p-value:	0.6671

Table E.2: Regression on log QSR-Inc

	Estimate	Std. Error	t value	Pr(> $\lvert t \rvert$)	
Completed ≥ 4 Years in Highschool-2nd Diff. L1	-0.0057	0.0129	-0.44	0.6595	
GDP Growth L1	0.0173	0.0100	1.73	0.0886	*
Unemployment Rate L1	0.0007	0.0060	0.12	0.9052	
GDP Deflator L1	0.0169	0.0324	0.52	0.6035	
Yield L1	-0.0228	0.0070	-3.25	0.0018	**
log QSR-Inc L1	0.5073	0.0732	6.93	0.0000	***
const	1.3626	0.2100	6.49	0.0000	***
trend	0.0011	0.0007	1.53	0.1296	
Variable Rupture	-0.2236	0.0357	-6.26	0.0000	***
Great Recession	0.0654	0.0303	2.16	0.0343	**
Signif. codes:	'***' 0.01 '**' 0.05 '*' 0.1				
Residual standard error:	0.05117 on 69 degrees of freedom				
Multiple R-squared:	0.9236,			Adjusted R-squared:	0.9136
JB-test, p-value:	Single regression:	0.8986	Multivariate:		0.5812
Portemanteau-test, pvalue:	0.23				
ARCH-test, p-value:	Single regression:	0.8092	Multivariate:		1
F-statistic:	92.62 on 9 and 69 DF,			p-value:	$< 2.2e-16$

Table E.3: Regression on log Variance-Inc

	Estimate	Std. Error	t value	Pr(> $\lvert t \rvert$)	
Completed ≥ 4 Years in Highschool-2nd Diff. L1	-0.0017	0.0269	-0.06	0.9490	
GDP Growth L1	0.0196	0.0198	0.99	0.3247	
Unemployment Rate L1	0.1031	0.0577	1.79	0.0788	*
GDP Deflator L1	-0.0034	0.0516	-0.07	0.9483	
Yield L1	0.0241	0.0190	1.27	0.2087	
log Variance-Inc L1	0.4455	0.1133	3.93	0.0002	***
Completed ≥ 4 Years in Highschool-2nd Diff. L2	0.0095	0.0261	0.36	0.7181	
GDP Growth L2	0.0180	0.0212	0.85	0.3995	
Unemployment Rate L2	-0.0955	0.0562	-1.70	0.0943	*
GDP Deflator L2	0.0972	0.0530	1.83	0.0715	*
Yield L2	-0.0314	0.0188	-1.67	0.0997	*
log Variance-Inc L2	0.1883	0.1243	1.51	0.1350	
const	6.2264	1.8634	3.34	0.0014	**
trend	0.0071	0.0021	3.30	0.0016	**
Variable Rupture	0.0202	0.0413	0.49	0.6270	
Great Recession	-0.0778	0.0491	-1.58	0.1182	
Signif. codes:	'***' 0.01 '**' 0.05 '*' 0.1				
Residual standard error:	1.304 on 62 degrees of freedom				
Multiple R-squared:	0.9669,			Adjusted R-squared:	0.9589
JB-test, p-value:	Single regression:	0.1919	Multivariate:		0.7776
Portemanteau-test, pvalue:	0.3893				
ARCH-test, p-value:	Single regression:	0.2953	Multivariate:		1
F-statistic:	120.7 on 15 and 62 DF,			p-value:	$< 2.2e-16$
F-statistic $H_0 : \begin{cases} \beta_{Yield.L1} = 0 \\ \beta_{Yield.L2} = 0 \end{cases}$	1.408 on 2 and 62 DF,			p-value:	0.2523
t-statistic $H_0 : \beta_{Yield.L1} + \beta_{Yield.L2} \geq 0$	-0.2020 on 62 DF,			p-value:	0.5797

Table E.4: Regression on RMPG-Exp

	Estimate	Std. Error	t value	Pr(> $\|t\|$)	
Completed ≥ 4 Years in Highschool-2nd Diff. L1	-0.1588	0.2678	-0.59	0.5549	
GDP Growth L1	0.0578	0.2388	0.24	0.8094	
Unemployment Rate L1	-0.2312	0.1340	-1.73	0.0884	*
FOR L1	-0.0747	0.1983	-0.38	0.7073	
GDP Deflator L1	-1.0872	0.6546	-1.66	0.1007	
Yield L1	0.0679	0.1541	0.44	0.6606	
RMPG-Exp L1	0.1281	0.1171	1.09	0.2774	
const	29.8033	5.3181	5.60	0.0000	***
trend	-0.0053	0.0062	-0.85	0.3959	
Great Recession	-0.6781	0.4886	-1.39	0.1691	
Signif. codes:	'*** 0.01 '**' 0.05 '*' 0.1				
Residual standard error:	1.168 on 78 degrees of freedom				
Multiple R-squared:	0.3351,			Adjusted R-squared:	0.2584
JB-test, p-value:	Single regression:	0.5063	Multivariate:		0.02682
Portemanteau-test, pvalue:	0.4595				
ARCH-test, p-value:	Single regression:	0.7336	Multivariate:		1
F-statistic:	4.368 on 9 and 78 DF,			p-value:	0.0001

Table E.5: Regression on log QSR-Exp

	Estimate	Std. Error	t value	Pr(> $\|t\|$)	
Completed ≥ 4 Years in Highschool-2nd Diff. L1	0.0030	0.0155	0.20	0.8450	
GDP Growth L1	-0.0111	0.0135	-0.82	0.4149	
Unemployment Rate L1	-0.0065	0.0074	-0.87	0.3872	
FOR L1	-0.0320	0.0133	-2.42	0.0184	**
GDP Deflator L1	-0.0398	0.0385	-1.03	0.3050	
Yield L1	-0.0052	0.0083	-0.62	0.5354	
$\log$ QSR-Exp L1	0.7437	0.0734	10.14	0.0000	***
const	1.3424	0.4000	3.36	0.0013	***
trend	-0.0021	0.0008	-2.51	0.0146	**
Great Recession	0.0388	0.0370	1.05	0.2979	
Signif. codes:	'*** 0.01 '**' 0.05 '*' 0.1				
Residual standard error:	0.0624 on 69 degrees of freedom				
Multiple R-squared:	0.8848,			Adjusted R-squared:	0.8697
JB-test, p-value:	Single regression:	$< 2.2e-16$	Multivariate:		$< 2.2e-16$
Portemanteau-test, pvalue:	0.4761				
ARCH-test, p-value:	Single regression:	0.9934	Multivariate:		1
F-statistic:	58.87 on 9 and 69 DF,			p-value:	$< 2.2e-16$

Table E.6: Regression on log Variance-Exp

	Estimate	Std. Error	t value	Pr(>|t|)	
Completed ≥ 4 Years in Highschool-2nd Diff. L1	0.0342	0.0689	0.50	0.6216	
GDP.growth.l1	-0.0038	0.0495	-0.08	0.9393	
Unemployment.Rate.l1	0.0270	0.1479	0.18	0.8556	
FOR.l1	-0.0704	0.1555	-0.45	0.6525	
GDP.Deflator.l1	-0.0106	0.1275	-0.08	0.9339	
Yield.l1	0.0151	0.0475	0.32	0.7524	
log.Variance.Exp.l1	-0.1231	0.1211	-1.02	0.3132	
Completed ≥ 4 Years in Highschool-2nd Diff. L2	-0.0527	0.0657	-0.80	0.4257	
GDP Growth L2	-0.0348	0.0528	-0.66	0.5116	
Unemployment Rate L2	-0.0239	0.1456	-0.16	0.8700	
FOR L2	0.1054	0.1459	0.72	0.4726	
GDP Deflator L2	0.2039	0.1293	1.58	0.1200	
Yield L2	-0.0837	0.0484	-1.73	0.0885	*
log Variance-Exp L2	-0.1017	0.1178	-0.86	0.3912	
const	18.9503	2.6121	7.25	0.0000	***
trend	0.0178	0.0034	5.19	0.0000	***
Great Recession	-0.3269	0.1253	-2.61	0.0114	**
Signif. codes:	'***' 0.01 '**' 0.05 '*' 0.1				
Residual standard error:	0.1936 on 61 degrees of freedom				
Multiple R-squared:	0.6357,			Adjusted R-squared:	0.5401
JB-test, p-value:	Single regression:	0.8117	Multivariate:		0.5702
Portemanteau-test, pvalue:	0.7291				
ARCH-test, p-value:	Single regression:	0.5751	Multivariate:		1
F-statistic:	6.653 on 16 and 61 DF,			p-value:	$2.302e-08$
F-statistic $H_0: \begin{cases}\beta_{Yield.L1}=0\\ \beta_{Yield.L2}=0\end{cases}$	3.2918 on 2 and 61 DF,			p-value:	0.0439
t-statistic $H_0: \beta_{Yield.L1}+\beta_{Yield.L2}\leq 0$	-0.7514 on 61 DF,			p-value:	0.2277

F Impulse Response Functions

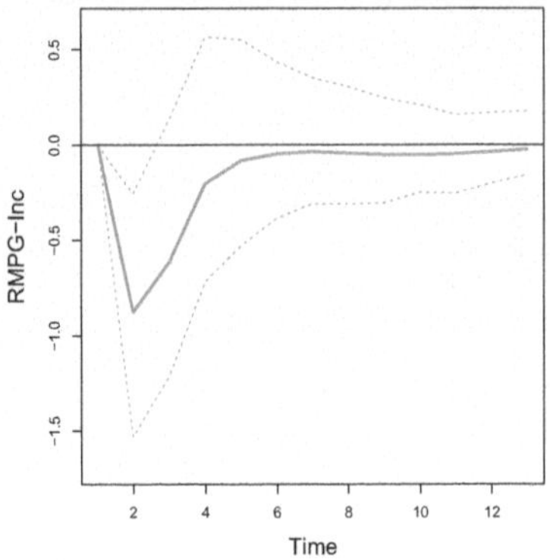

Figure F.1: IRF of Yield on RMPG-Inc

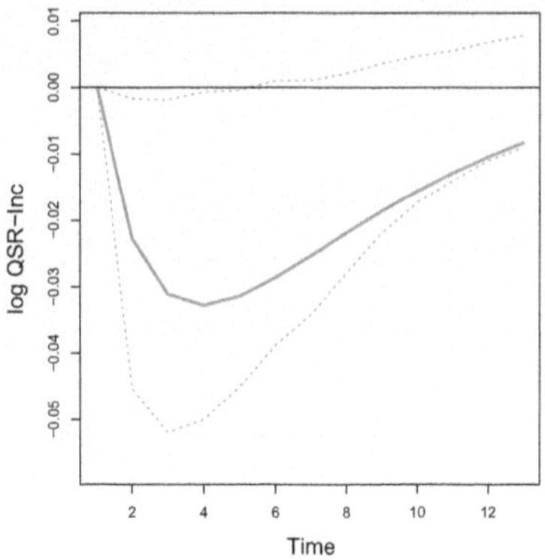

Figure F.2: IRF of Yield on log QSR-Inc

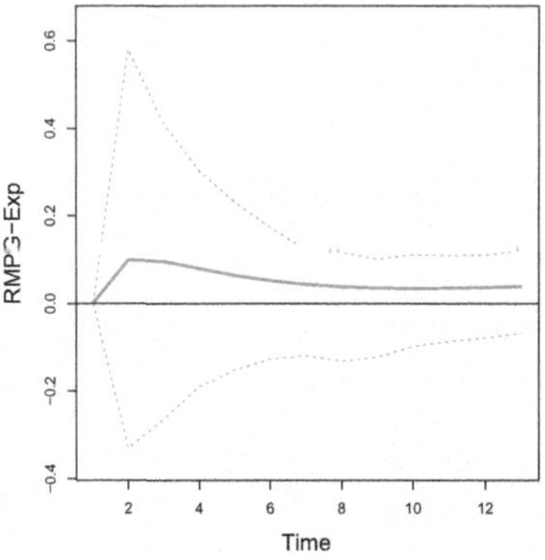

Figure F.3: IRF of Yield on RMPG-Exp

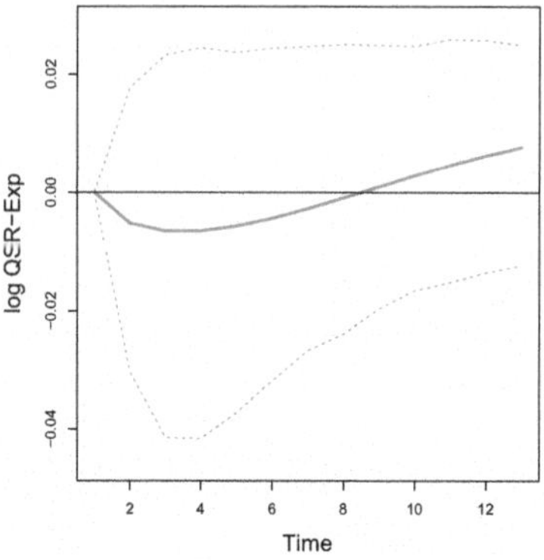

Figure F.4: IRF of Yield on log QSR-Exp

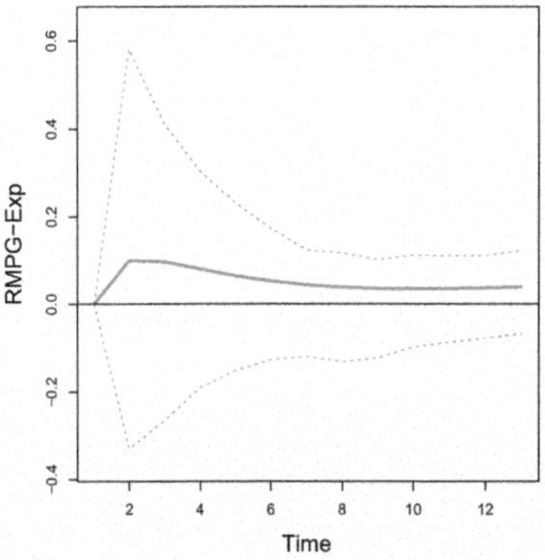

Figure F.5: IRF of Yield on log Variance-Exp

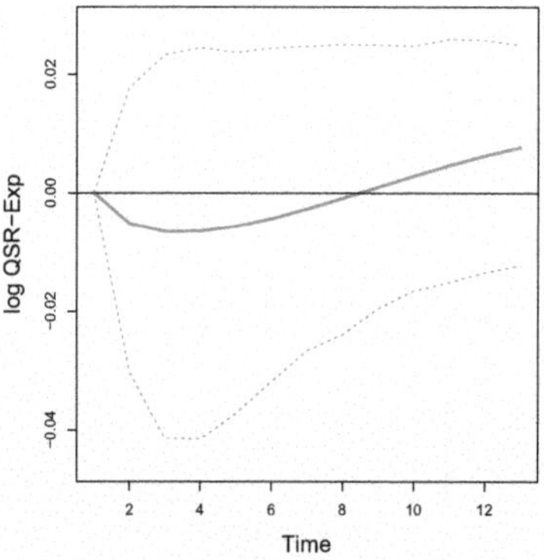

Figure F.6: IRF of Inflation on log Variance-Exp

The manufacturer's authorised representative in the EU is Springer Nature Customer Service Centre GmbH, Europaplatz 3, 69115 Heidelberg, Germany. If you have any concerns regarding our products, please contact ProductSafety@springernature.com

Printed and bound by CPI Group (UK) Ltd, Croydon, CR0 4YY
01/10/2026
02226496-0001